CliffsNotes™

Hinton's
The Outsiders

By Janet Clark

IN THIS BOOK

- Learn about the Life and Background of the Author
- Preview an Introduction to the Novel
- Explore themes, character development, and recurring images in the Critical Commentaries
- Examine in-depth Character Analyses
- Acquire an understanding of the novel with Critical Essays
- Reinforce what you learn with CliffsNotes Review
- Find additional information to further your study in the CliffsNotes Resource Center and online at www.cliffsnotes.com

D0289962

IDG Books Worldwide, Inc.
An International Data Group Company
Foster City, CA • Chicago, IL • Indianapolis, IN • New York, NY

About the Author

Janet Clark is a certified elementary education teacher who has taught in an inner-city Kansas City school, a rural Nebraska one-room school house, and in the People's Republic of China. She is currently the School-Age Coordinator for a United Way agency in Lincoln, Nebraska.

Publisher's Acknowledgments

Editorial

Project Editor: Alissa Cayton
Acquisitions Editor: Greg Tubach
Senior Copy Editor: Susan Diane Smith
Glossary Editors: The editors and staff of Webster's New World Dictionaries
Editorial Administrator: Michelle Hacker

Production

Indexer: York Production Services, Inc.
Proofreader: York Production Services, Inc.
IDG Books Indianapolis Production Department

CliffsNotes™ Hinton's *The Outsiders*

Published by
IDG Books Worldwide, Inc.
An International Data Group Company
919 E. Hillsdale Blvd.
Suite 400
Foster City, CA 94404

www.idgbooks.com (IDG Books Worldwide Web site)

www.cliffsnotes.com (CliffsNotes Web site)

ISBN: 0-7645-8559-2

Printed in the United States of America

10 9 8 7 6 5 4 3 2 1

1V/ST/QV/QQ/IN

Distributed in the United States by IDG Books Worldwide, Inc.

Distributed by CDG Books Canada Inc. for Canada; by Transworld Publishers Limited in the United Kingdom; by IDG Norge Books for Norway; by IDG Sweden Books for Sweden; by IDG Books Australia Publishing Corporation Pty. Ltd. for Australia and New Zealand; by TransQuest Publishers Pte Ltd. for Singapore, Malaysia, Thailand, Indonesia, and Hong Kong; by Gotop Information Inc. for Taiwan; by ICG Muse, Inc. for Japan; by Intersoft for South Africa; by Eyrolles for France; by International Thomson Publishing for Germany, Austria and Switzerland; by Distribuidora Cuspide for Argentina; by LR International for Brazil; by Galileo Libros for Chile; by Ediciones ZETA S.C.R. Ltda. for Peru; by WS Computer Publishing Corporation, Inc., for the Philippines; by Contemporanea de Ediciones for Venezuela; by Express Computer Distributors for the Caribbean and West Indies; by Micronesia Media Distributor, Inc. for Micronesia; by Chips Computadoras S.A. de C.V. for Mexico; by Editorial Norma de Panama S.A. for Panama; by American Bookshops for Finland.

For general information on IDG Books Worldwide's books in the U.S., please call our Consumer Customer Service department at **800-762-2974**. For reseller information, including discounts and premium sales, please call our Reseller Customer Service department at **800-434-3422**.

For information on where to purchase IDG Books Worldwide's books outside the U.S., please contact our International Sales department at **317-596-5530** or fax **317-572-4002**.

For consumer information on foreign language translations, please contact our Customer Service department at **800-434-3422**, fax 317-572-4002, or e-mail rights@idgbooks.com.

For information on licensing foreign or domestic rights, please phone **650-653-7098**.

For sales inquiries and special prices for bulk quantities, please contact our Order Services department at **800-434-3422** or write to the address above.

For information on using IDG Books Worldwide's books in the classroom or for ordering examination copies, please contact our Educational Sales department at **800-434-2086** or fax **317-572-4005**.

For press review copies, author interviews, or other publicity information, please contact our Public Relations department at **650-653-7000** or fax **650-653-7500**.

For authorization to photocopy items for corporate, personal, or educational use, please contact Copyright Clearance Center, 222 Rosewood Drive, Danvers, MA 01923, or fax **978-750-4470**.

Note: If you purchased this book without a cover, you should be aware that this book is stolen property. It was reported as "unsold and destroyed" to the publisher, and neither the author nor the publisher has received any payment for this "stripped book."

Library of Congress Cataloging-in-Publication Data

Author, First Name.
    CliffsNotes, Hinton's The Outsiders / by Janet Clark.
        p. cm.
    Includes index.
    ISBN 0-7645-8559-2 (alk. paper)
    1. Hinton, S. E. Outsiders--Examinations--Study guides. I. Title: Outsiders. II. Title.

PS3558.I548 O984 2000
813'.54--dc21   00-039693
                                                    CIP

Table of Contents

How to Use This Book

CliffsNotes Hinton's *The Outsiders* supplements the original work, giving you background information about the author, an introduction to the novel, a graphical character map, critical commentaries, expanded glossaries, and a comprehensive index. CliffsNotes Review tests your comprehension of the original text and reinforces learning with questions and answers, practice projects, and more. For further information on S. E. Hinton and *The Outsiders*, check out the CliffsNotes Resource Center.

CliffsNotes provides the following icons to highlight essential elements of particular interest:

 Reveals the underlying themes in the work.

 Helps you to more easily relate to or discover the depth of a character.

 Uncovers elements such as setting, atmosphere, mystery, passion, violence, irony, symbolism, tragedy, foreshadowing, and satire.

 Enables you to appreciate the nuances of words and phrases.

Don't Miss Our Web Site

Discover classic literature as well as modern-day treasures by visiting the CliffsNotes Web site at www.cliffsnotes.com. You can obtain a quick download of a CliffsNotes title, purchase a title in print form, browse our catalog, or view online samples.

You'll also find interactive tools that are fun and informative, links to interesting Web sites, tips, articles, and additional resources to help you, not only for literature, but for test prep, finance, careers, computers, and the Internet too. See you at www.cliffsnotes.com!

LIFE AND BACKGROUND OF THE AUTHOR

Personal Background

Susan Eloise Hinton was born in 1950 in Tulsa, Oklahoma. *The Outsiders* was published in 1967, when Hinton was only 17 years old and attending Will Rogers High School. She began writing the first draft of the novel when she was 15, and writing and rewriting took a year and a half before she was happy with the final copy.

The publisher—believing that the book would have more credibility if people assumed that a male had written it—advised her to use her initials, S. E.

Early Years

Hinton was not a member of a gang when she wrote *The Outsiders*, but she was a friend to many greasers. She has stated that her biggest compliment was that her greaser friends liked the book. Although she also had friends who were Socs, she definitely did not consider herself a part of that group. Her mother's reaction to the novel was shock; she said, "Susie, where did you pick up all of this?"

Education

The success of *The Outsiders* enabled Hinton to attend the University of Tulsa where she earned a degree in education in 1970. However, during her student teaching, she decided that she did not have the physical stamina to be a teacher. She found herself teaching all day and then worrying about the kids all night.

Hinton did meet her future husband, David Inhofe, in a freshman biology class, and it was due to him that she finished her second book, *That Was Then, This is Now*. Hinton was suffering from writer's block, and he forced her to write two pages a day. If she failed to produce two pages during the day, they wouldn't go out that night. They were married in 1970, and *That Was Then, This is Now* was published in 1971.

Publication History

Hinton considers her second book, *That Was Then, This Is Now,* to be better written than *The Outsiders*. It is about two 16-year-old friends, Mark and Byron, who are like brothers. However, they find their lives pulling apart due to involvement with girls, gangs, and drugs.

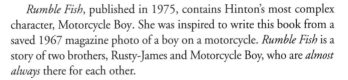

Rumble Fish, published in 1975, contains Hinton's most complex character, Motorcycle Boy. She was inspired to write this book from a saved 1967 magazine photo of a boy on a motorcycle. *Rumble Fish* is a story of two brothers, Rusty-James and Motorcycle Boy, who are *almost always* there for each other.

Hinton's next book, *Tex*, published in 1980, is about two delinquent brothers left on their own by a rambling father. In 1982, Disney Studios released *Tex*, and Hinton agreed to the movie deal with the condition that her horse got to play the lead horse in the movie.

Taming the Star Runner was book number five and a departure from her usual story-telling technique. This story about a brave young girl taming her horse is told in the third person. With the completion of this novel, Hinton took a seven-year break in her writing to concentrate on her only child, Nick.

Big David, Little David and *The Puppy Sister* were both published in 1995 and are children's books. *Big David, Little David* is a picture book that was conceived from a joke that her husband played on their child. Hinton considers *The Puppy Sister* to be her most autobiographical work, because it is about her son and the sibling rivalry that existed between him and their puppy.

Honors and Awards

S. E. Hinton has received numerous honors and awards. She won the Margaret Alexander Edwards Award in 1988. This award honors authors "whose book or books, over a period of time, have been accepted by young people as an authentic voice that continues to illuminate their experiences and emotions, giving insight into their lives."

S. E. Hinton has won the following awards for her first novel, *The Outsiders:*

- *New York Herald Tribune* Best Teenage Books List, 1967

- *Chicago Tribune* Book World Spring Book Festival Honor Book, 1967

- Media and Methods Maxi Award, 1975

- American Library Association Best Young Adults Books, 1975

- Massachusetts Children's Book Award, 1979

Hinton received the following awards for *That Was Then, This Is Now:*

- American Library Association Best Books for Young Adults, 1971

- *Chicago Tribune* Book World Spring Book Festival Honor Book, 1971

- Massachusetts Children's Book Award, 1978

Hinton won these awards for *Rumble Fish:*

- American Library Association Best Books for Young Adults, 1975

- *School Library Journal* Best Books of the Year, 1975

Hinton has received the following awards for *Tex:*

- American Library Association Best Books for Young Adults, 1979

- *School Library Journal* Best Books of the Year, 1979

- New York Public Library Books for the Teen Age, 1980

- American Book Award Nomination, 1981

- Sue Hefly Honor Book, Louisiana Association of School Librarians, 1982

- California Young Reader Medal Nomination, 1982

- Sue Hefly Award, Louisiana Association of School Librarians, 1983

INTRODUCTION TO THE NOVEL

Introduction

The Outsiders was written by a teenager about teenagers. It is told in a first-person narration style, with the narrator being a 14-year-old boy. This story deals with issues that are very close to the hearts of teens, whether in the 1960s when this book was written or today.

Ponyboy Curtis is the narrator of this story, and it is through his eyes that the events unfold. Ponyboy takes the reader through a two-week period that will shape the rest of his life. No adults figure prominently in this novel; Pony and his two brothers are living on their own because their parents were recently killed in an automobile accident. But this story—which was written by a teen and focuses only on teens—touches every adult who reads it because the emotions and struggles the characters face are universal.

This novel is set in the 1960s in Oklahoma. The time period of the story is the same as the actual time it was written. The references that allow the reader to determine the era are cultural: popular musicians, television shows, and models of cars. To know the time period helps readers understand some of the references, but it is not critical to understanding the story. The fact that it is in Oklahoma is not necessarily a strong ingredient for the success of the story either. The author makes multiple references to rodeos and basic horsemanship, but those details are not as relevant as the fact that the story is set in a semi-large city. Walking from the East Side to the West side would take approximately 20 minutes, according to the text, and from that information readers can infer the size.

One of the most important qualities that can help teens establish their own identities is the ability to "fit in." Finding friends who understand their problems and relate to them is paramount for teenagers.

The novel is built around the class division between the *Socs,* ("the abbreviation for the Socials, the jet set, the West-side rich kids") and the *greasers* (a term that refers to the "boys on the East Side," who are "poorer than the Socs and the middle class"). The members of many small neighborhood gangs identify themselves as greasers.

The main characters in *The Outsiders*—Ponyboy Curtis, Darry Curtis, Sodapop Curtis, Two-Bit Mathews, Steve Randle, Dally Winston, and Johnny Cade—make up a small gang of greasers.

Two themes that run throughout this novel are intricately linked with gang philosophy.

Belonging to a gang instantly gives a teen an extended family. And that family automatically understands him, which is usually different from the family into which he was born. Gang membership also means that you are accepted. You are not an outsider; you are on the inside with at least one group.

Life isn't fair. The idea that life isn't fair is based entirely on one's perspective. Whether life is unfair to the greasers (the main characters' perspective) or to the Socs, (the rival groups' perspective) is a question that is recurrent in the novel. Rarely is injustice seen equally by all eyes.

A third theme that runs throughout this novel is one of colors in a black and white world. Hinton does an excellent job of painting verbal pictures. She uses contrasting colors to not only give impressions, but also to add depth to the story. Teens are often quick to see only right or wrong in a situation. But nothing is ever that cut and dried. Using colors, Hinton allows the reader to visualize the extremes and then mix them together to show that there is a middle ground. This theme is not the most important element in the story, but it is a good literary technique that allows the reader to visualize the story and internalize the intensity of the feelings that run strong in adolescents.

The Outsiders can be termed a coming-of-age novel because of the many topics that the story deals with.

Cigarette smoking, like many serious issues, is treated in the novel as part of everyday life. Several reasons may explain the author's approach to smoking: The Surgeon General's report linking cigarette smoking to cancer had just come out in 1964 and the implications were not widely realized; the author may have believed that, inevitably, some teenagers experiment with smoking; or perhaps cigarettes were just a prop to help readers better visualize the characters. Whatever the reason, the treatment of the subject did not affect the telling of the story. The importance, or lack of it, was even underscored when the main character, Ponyboy, who is only 14, is surprised when an adult tells him that he shouldn't be smoking.

Suicide, a hot topic among teens, is not glossed over. One of the main characters had often considered suicide, and not until he is dying from other injuries does he regret considering that action. Hinton tries to impress upon readers that teenagers may not have the perspective to understand that life is short enough already and they have so much to see and do in the future.

Teen pregnancy receives attention in the book. The way Hinton handles teen pregnancy may seem outdated. When the girlfriend of one of Ponyboy's brothers becomes pregnant, she is immediately shipped off to live with family in Texas. This consequence undoubtedly still happens today, but it is not the norm. With child-care centers in most large high schools, the social stigma attached to teen motherhood no longer exists as it did in the 1960s.

Underage drinking is common throughout the book. An author writing today might treat the issue of drinking and driving differently than Hinton did in the 1960s. In this book, the teens who are drinking are often driving. One character, Cherry Valance, condemns adults and questions their motives when they sell alcohol to minors, but teen drinking isn't meant to be the focus of the book.

The importance of remaining in school and graduating recurs throughout the novel, but that topic is also not meant to be a primary focus.

These issues make the story interesting, and Hinton does a very good job at not preaching at the reader. If this story had been written without touching on at least some of these topics, it would lack realism.

Hinton allows readers to take an active role in this story. She effectively utilizes foreshadowing and almost challenges the reader to anticipate what is coming next. This technique works well because it does not distract readers from the story's action; it encourages critical thought and increases anticipation. The fact that this story ends with the same line that it opens with creates a full circle. This twist prompts the reader to read the book again, this time discovering that the outcome is within Ponyboy all of the time, it just literally needs to be spelled out for us, the reader.

A Brief Synopsis

The Outsiders is about two weeks in the life of a 14-year-old boy. The novel tells the story of Ponyboy Curtis and his struggles with right and wrong in a society in which he believes that he is an outsider.

Ponyboy and his two brothers—Darrel (Darry), who is 20, and Sodapop, who is 16—have recently lost their parents in an automobile accident. Pony and Soda are allowed to stay under Darry's guardianship as long as they all behave themselves. The boys are greasers, a class term that refers to the young men on the East Side, the poor side of town. The greasers' rivals are the Socs, short for Socials, who are the "Westside rich kids."

The story opens with Pony walking home alone from a movie; he is stopped by a gang of Socs who proceed to beat him up. The Socs badly injure and threaten to kill Ponyboy; however, some of his gang happen upon the scene and run the Socs off. This incident sets the tone for the rest of the story, because the event tells the reader that a fight between these two groups needs no provocation.

The next night Pony and two other gang members, Dallas Winston (Dally) and Johnny Cade, go to a drive-in movie. There they meet Sherri (Cherry) Valance and her friend Marcia, who have left their Soc boyfriends at the drive-in because the boys were drinking. Dally leaves after giving the girls a hard time, but another greaser, Two-Bit Mathews, joins Pony and Johnny. The boys offer to walk the girls home after the movie, but along the way, the girls' boyfriends reappear and threaten to fight the greasers. Cherry stops the fight from happening, and the girls leave with their boyfriends.

Pony and Johnny go to a vacant lot to hang out before heading home. They fall asleep, and when Johnny wakes Pony up it's 2 a.m. Pony runs home, because the time is way past his curfew, and Darry is waiting up. Darry is furious with Pony and, in the heat of the moment, he hits him. Pony runs out of the house and returns to the lot to find Johnny. Pony wants to run away, but instead they go to the park to cool off before heading back home.

At the park, Cherry's and Marcia's boyfriends reappear. Pony and Johnny are outnumbered, and the Socs grab Ponyboy and shove him face first into the fountain, holding his head under the water. Realizing that Ponyboy is drowning, Johnny panics, pulls his switchblade, and kills the Soc, Bob.

Ponyboy and Johnny seek out Dally for help in running away to avoid being arrested for Bob's murder. He gives them $50 and directions to a hideout outside of town. The boys hop a freight train and find the hideout where they are to wait until Dally comes for them. Hiding in an abandoned, rural church, they feel like real outsiders, with their greased, long hair and general hoody appearance. They both cut their hair, and Pony colors his for a disguise. They pass the time in the church playing cards and reading aloud from *Gone with the Wind*.

Dally shows up after a week, and takes them to the Dairy Queen in Windrixville. Thanks to Dally, the police think that the boys are headed for Texas. Dally also brings them the news that Cherry Valance is now being a spy for the greasers, and helping them out against the Socs. She has also testified that Bob was drunk the night of his death and that she was sure that the killing had been in self-defense.

Johnny decides that he has a chance now, and announces that he wants to turn himself in. They head back to the church and discover that it is on fire. A school group is there, apparently on some kind of outing, and little kids are trapped inside. Without thinking, Pony and Johnny race inside and rescue the kids. As they are handing the kids outside to Dally, the burning roof collapses. Pony barely escapes, but a piece of timber falls on Johnny, burning him badly and breaking his back. The boys, now viewed as heroes, are taken via ambulance back to town, where Pony reunites with his brothers.

Johnny dies of his injuries. Dally is overcome with grief, and he robs a grocery store. He flees the police and calls the gang from a telephone booth, asking them to pick him up in the vacant lot and take him to a hiding place. The police chase Dally to the lot, and as the gang watches, Dally pulls a "black object" from his waistband and the officers shoot him.

The senselessness of all the violent events traumatizes Pony, but he deals with his grief and frustration by writing this book for all of the "Dallys" in the world.

List of Characters

Ponyboy Michael Curtis A 14-year-old boy who is the narrator and main character in *The Outsiders*. His parents have been killed in an automobile accident, and he lives with his two brothers.

Soda(pop) Patrick Curtis Ponyboy's 16-going-on-17-year-old brother. He is a high school dropout and works at the local gas station. He is "movie-star" handsome.

Darrel (Darry) Shayne Curtis The 20-year-old brother and legal guardian of Ponyboy and Soda. He works too hard and too long, and would be in college, if life had turned out different.

Dallas (Dally) Winston A fellow greaser, who is originally from New York City. He is a bit tougher than the others in Ponyboy's gang, and at 17 he has already seen the inside of a jail.

Johnny Cade The "gang's pet." He is 16 years old, physically small, and comes from a physically and verbally abusive home. Dally is his hero.

Steve Randle Soda's best friend and fellow greaser. He is 17 and works at the gas station with Soda.

Keith (Two-Bit) Mathews The oldest of the gang, except for Darry, and still a junior in high school at age 18. He is the wise-cracking comedian of the gang.

Sherri (Cherry) Valance A cheerleader and the girlfriend of Bob, the Soc who is killed. Cherry and Ponyboy meet at the drive-in and become friends. Cherry is attracted to Dally, and becomes a spy for the greasers.

Marcia Cherry's girlfriend at the drive-in. She gives Two-Bit her phone number, but he throws it away.

Bob Sheldon The Soc who originally attacked Johnny, and then attacks both Johnny and Pony in the park. Johnny Cade kills Bob during an altercation when some Socs try to drown Ponyboy.

Randy Adderson The owner of the blue Mustang that haunts Johnny. He is Bob's best friend and fellow Soc.

Tim Shepard A fellow greaser, but not a member of the main characters' gang. His greaser gang is rougher, and the members are termed "future convicts." He is both Dally's main rival and friend.

Jerry Wood The overweight man at the church fire. He rides along with Pony in the ambulance and calls the boys heroes. Pony confides everything to him, and he still calls them heroes.

Buck Merril Dally's rodeo partner, a man in his mid 20s. Johnny and Pony find Dally at Buck's party. Buck loans Dally his T-Bird.

Character Map

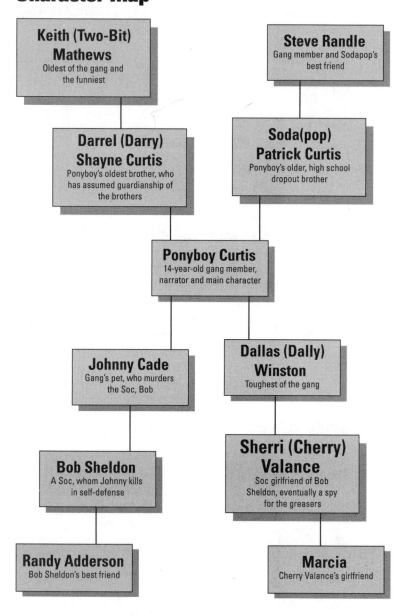

Keith (Two-Bit) Mathews
Oldest of the gang and the funniest

Steve Randle
Gang member and Sodapop's best friend

Darrel (Darry) Shayne Curtis
Ponyboy's oldest brother, who has assumed guardianship of the brothers

Soda(pop) Patrick Curtis
Ponyboy's older, high school dropout brother

Ponyboy Curtis
14-year-old gang member, narrator and main character

Johnny Cade
Gang's pet, who murders the Soc, Bob

Dallas (Dally) Winston
Toughest of the gang

Bob Sheldon
A Soc, whom Johnny kills in self-defense

Sherri (Cherry) Valance
Soc girlfriend of Bob Sheldon, eventually a spy for the greasers

Randy Adderson
Bob Sheldon's best friend

Marcia
Cherry Valance's girlfriend

CRITICAL COMMENTARIES

Chapter 1

Summary

The Outsiders is narrated by the main character, Ponyboy Curtis. The story is placed in Oklahoma during the 1960s.

In the first chapter, Ponyboy introduces himself and gives a brief history of his family. He also describes the relationships between his gang members, and the relationships within his own family. Ponyboy's parents were killed in an automobile accident, leaving him and his two brothers on their own.

Ponyboy is the youngest at 14, Sodapop is 16, and Darry is 20. The authorities allow the three brothers to stay together as long as they "behave." Ponyboy resents Darry and the total control that he attempts to wield over his life; he views their relationship as adversarial and looks to Sodapop for understanding and love.

The brothers consider their gang members—Steve Randle, Two-Bit Mathews, Dallas Winston, and Johnny Cade—to be family. All of the members come from dysfunctional homes and need the gang relationship as a substitute for what is missing in their own families.

As Ponyboy walks home alone after going to a movie, he realizes the inherent danger of doing so. He explains to the reader that he is a greaser, a term "used to class all us boys on the East Side," which is the poor side of town. Greasers are known for their long, greased hair. Walking home alone is dangerous because the rival gang, the Socs, could easily attack him. The Socs, short for Socials, are "the jet set, the West-side rich kids," who are from upper-middle-class families. Ponyboy explains that the gangs are "just small bunches of friends who stick together, and the warfare is between the social classes."

As if foreshadowing Ponyboy's own poor decision to walk alone, a carload of four Socs arrives, and one pulls a knife on him. As he attempts to fend off his attackers, Ponyboy hears the pounding of footsteps and the attack turns into an all-out fight as his gang arrives to rescue him from the Socs' attack. Ponyboy's two brothers, Darry and Sodapop, along with their four other gang members, chase the Socs away; Ponyboy escapes with cuts and bruises.

Commentary

The narration of this story by a 14-year-old boy allows for the novel to be written in an easy-to-read format.

Theme

The first chapter introduces three major themes immediately.

An outsider's view. Many of the characters feel like outsiders and believe that life isn't fair to them, but the novel shows that the reality is a matter of perspective. Whether someone defines himself or herself as an outsider or insider depends on his or her personal perspective or viewpoint. Life from an outsider's perspective is not only one of the main themes, but the one for which the novel is named.

An outsider sees things differently than someone who is directly involved in a way of life. The East Side greasers are "outsiders" to the West side of town, the "rich" side. To an outsider, West-side life can look very appealing, but it is unappreciated by the Socs who live there. Ponyboy says of the greasers, "We're poorer than the Socs and the middle class. I reckon we're wilder, too. Not like the Socs, who jump greasers and wreck houses and throw beer blasts for kicks. . . ."

Someone who always feels like an outsider may conclude that life is unfair. Pony and the rest of the greasers must deal with the hardship in their own lives, while the Socs enjoy all the advantages of class privilege. This "life isn't fair" theme is prevalent throughout the book and concerns the issue of inclusion versus exclusion, of fitting in. The idea that life is not fair is a matter of perspective.

In this chapter, Ponyboy analyzes the Socs' lives through his own eyes, an outsider's perspective, which can only see and understand one view. After the Socs attack Pony, he thinks, "I had just as much right to use the streets as the Socs did, and Johnny had never hurt them. Why did the Socs hate us so much?"

Realistic family love. Family love and the intricate relationships that are forged therein is another theme touched on in Chapter 1. During adolescence, many people begin to examine their own roles in their family structures. Ponyboy's relationship with his two brothers symbolizes the traditional dual-parent relationship. Darry has taken over the role of the father, the disciplinarian and the rule maker; Ponyboy even notes a physical resemblance between his real father and Darry. Sodapop has become the nurturing mother; he always sticks up for Ponyboy and tries to explain Darry's love for him.

Also an issue within any family is an individual's own expectations of other family members. For example, in the novel, Darry wants Ponyboy to get all A's and expects nothing less. However, Ponyboy wants Darry to be supportive, regardless of the grades he receives.

Colors in a black and white world. This theme focuses on a teenager's tendency to see only the extremes of an issue, not the gray areas. This idea underscores many issues that affect an adolescent's life.

The third theme of colors in a black and white world is important in building the depth of the novel. Teens often see only two sides—black and white—of every issue. The author's use of colors not only helps the characters begin to see the middle range, but also enables the reader to discover the many layers in this book. Describing Dally, Hinton alludes to the color range: "The shade of difference that separates a greaser from a hood wasn't present in Dally."

Hinton descriptively stresses the colors of the characters' eyes, hair, and even clothing, as well as their environment. Generally, she associates warm colors with the Socs and cool colors with the greasers. Warmth usually is equated with inside and cool is associated with outside, and the colors reflect the characters' positions in society: The greasers view the Socs as insiders and themselves as outsiders.

The cool colors representative of Ponyboy's gang emphasize that they are continually forced to be outsiders looking in.

In Hinton's original descriptions of Ponyboy's gang, she uses primarily cool colors. Ponyboy's eyes are greenish-gray, Darry's eyes "are like two pieces of pale blue-green ice," Dally's hair "was almost white it was so blond" and his eyes are "blue, blazing ice, cold with a hatred," and Two-Bit Mathews has gray eyes. However, in describing Soda, she acknowledges that his hair color changes in the summertime. "He's got dark-gold hair that . . . in the summer the sun bleaches it to a shining wheat-gold." This description shows change, and the color combinations that are in the middle, not the extremes.

By giving readers such extreme details of hair and eye coloration, the author suggests that perhaps the greasers primarily see the world through a filter of chilling inequity.

A minor theme prevalent throughout Western literature and established here in Chapter 1 is the power of three. This is a dominant theme found in many fairy tales and much folklore, and thus it makes sense that it would also appear in the narration of a story told by a 14-year-old boy.

Hinton introduces the theme here with the three brothers. Together they have the strength to be a family and face the challenges that the world offers. Note that as the novel opens, Ponyboy, one of the three brothers, is alone and thus more vulnerable than if he were with his two brothers.

Glossary

Paul Newman (b. 1925) popular actor known for his good looks and blue eyes.

Corvair a Chevrolet automobile model.

madras a fine, firm cotton cloth, usually striped or plaid, used for shirts, dresses, and so on.

Will Rogers (born *William Penn Adair Rogers*) (1879–1935) U.S. humorist and actor.

the cooler [Slang] jail.

savvy [Slang] to understand; get the idea.

Chapter 2

Summary

Ponyboy and Johnny meet up with Dally (Dallas) and go to the Nightly Double drive-in theatre. They sneak into the drive-in, although the admission is only 25 cents if you're without a car. They enjoy the challenge of sneaking in because Dally hates to do anything the legal way. Once inside, they sit in the chairs by the concession stand, where they meet up with two good-looking female Socs. Cherry (Sherri) Valance and Marcia have left their boyfriends here at the drive-in because the boy's want to drink and the two girls do not. The girls are the target of Dally's nasty and rude comments, but he buys them sodas to "cool them off." Cherry throws her soda into Dally's face and the situation is tense until Johnny steps in to defend her, which is surprising given that Johnny worships Dally and considers him his hero. Fortunately, Johnny is the gangs' pet, so Dally just stalks off without confrontation. Two-Bit joins Ponyboy and Johnny, and he and Marcia hit it off.

Cherry is impressed with Johnny's courage, but she senses something else in Johnny. She quizzes Ponyboy about Johnny. Cherry's accurate assessment that Johnny's "been hurt bad sometime" prompts Ponyboy to retell the story of Johnny's beating by the Socs. About four months ago, Johnny was out in a field hunting a football to practice a few kicks, and four Socs drove by in a blue Mustang. They stopped and jumped him, beating Johnny half to death. One of the Socs wore several rings and the rings badly cut Johnny. The beating wasn't what had changed Johnny, it was the fact that they had scared him. Johnny never walked alone anymore, and he vowed that he would kill the next person who jumped him.

The story of Johnny's beating visibly upsets Cherry. She tells Ponyboy that not all Socs are like that, just like all greasers are not like Dally. She tells him that Socs have their troubles, too, but Ponyboy cannot imagine what worries a Soc might have. The chapter concludes with the line, "I know better now."

Commentary

Theme

    This chapter introduces the importance of perspective. The lament that life isn't fair runs throughout this chapter, but now a Soc also brings it forth. Cherry Valance represents the perfect life to Ponyboy. She is a good-looking cheerleader, but she states that the Socs have troubles, too. Her life appears perfect to an outsider looking in, but that apparently is not the case.

    After listening to the story of Johnny's beating, Cherry does not feel a need to defend the Socs who attacked Johnny, but she feels the need to qualify the fact that not only the greasers have difficulties: "@'We have troubles you've never even heard of. You want to know something?' She looked me straight in the eye. 'Things are rough all over.'" Ponyboy states that he believes her, but he later confides to the reader that he doubts her outlook. This viewpoint is a measure of his perspective that readers can watch grow and change as the novel continues.

    The gang is defined again as family: "When you're a gang, you stick up for the members. If you don't stick up for them, stick together, make like brothers, it isn't a gang anymore." This extended family is a very important element of safety. Seemingly, none of the families represented by Ponyboy's gang have stuck together. Whether because of death (in Ponyboy's case), the departure of a parent or child (in Dally's case), divorce, or child abuse, the greasers are searching for a family atmosphere that supports them. Within the gang, the notion of sticking together, of one unified *all*, is one of the most important rules. Pony sincerely believes that it's the gang's responsibility to defend one another. The code of honor that protects Ponyboy's gang is held by all: "When you're a gang, you stick up for the members."

    The gang rule that members must stick together is also part of the driving force of Ponyboy's family. The boys must stick together if they are going to make it on their own—that is, without adult supervision. Ponyboy continues to struggle with the expectations that he holds for his own family members.

    Pony craves unconditional love and support from Darry; he also wants Darry to trust that he will do the right thing, not berate him for his lack of common sense. The fact that Soda is a high school dropout is very disturbing to Pony. He feels that Soda is not living up to his potential and is embarrassed by it: "I never have gotten over that. I could hardly stand it when he left school."

Cherry knows Sodapop, because he works at the gas station, and she asks why she hasn't seen him in school. Ponyboy is embarrassed to admit that Soda is a dropout. This admission "made me think of some poor dumb-looking hoodlum wandering the streets breaking out street lights—it didn't fit my happy-go-lucky brother at all."

The name Cherry Valance is great fun. The word *cherry* can be slang for both perfect and red. Cherry is a Soc and she is perfect in Ponyboy's eyes. The fact that "cherry" also means red highlights the author's use of color as a theme in the book. She associates warm colors with Socs and cool colors with greasers. Warmth usually is associated with inside and cool with outside. The colors represent the groups' positions in society: The greasers view the Socs as insiders and themselves as outsiders.

Hinton uses the color white twice in this chapter to describe fright. Initially, she uses the color to describe Johnny at the drive-in when Two-Bit surprises him by sneaking up behind him and impersonating a Soc. Hinton also describes Cherry as "white as a sheet" after listening to Ponyboy's version of Johnny's attack. The use of this color as an apt description for both groups continues the merging of colors. The world is not quite so black and white when the colors begin to cross lines.

The final sentence of the chapter tips the reader off that the narration technique is retrospective. Ponyboy is retelling this story and is, therefore, able to include foreshadowing, which not only teases readers, but allows them to witness his character's growth.

During Chapter 2, Pony's character is not able to see Cherry's point of view that the Socs have their own troubles. But the last sentence of the chapter, "I know better now," not only foreshadows upcoming events, but also shows Ponyboy's own personal growth. Later, he develops a better understanding of the Socs and changes his own perspective. With hindsight, in the retelling of this story, he is able to see the Socs in a different light: "I really couldn't see what Socs would have to sweat about—good grades, good cars, good girls, madras and Mustangs and Corvairs." This sentence was written in the past tense, "really couldn't see," with an implied correction of understanding. This notes a change in Ponyboy's perspective.

Foreshadowing is heavy within Johnny's story. This tale of injustice reveals the impact that the beating by the Socs four months ago had on Johnny's life. The physical wounds have healed but his terror is still obvious. The emotional scars that Johnny is left with from this beating are almost a roadmap to his destiny. Ponyboy says of Johnny, "He would kill the next person who jumped him. Nobody was ever going to beat him like that again." This statement foreshadows the later attack by the Socs. In the life of a greaser, it is inevitable that another fight will take place.

Glossary

the fuzz [Slang] a policeman or the police.

chessy cat [Slang] Cheshire cat, a proverbial grinning cat from Cheshire, England, especially one described in Lewis Carroll's *Alice's Adventures in Wonderland.*

weed [Informal] a cigar or cigarette.

Chapter 3

Summary

The movie comes to an end and the group decides to walk over to Two-Bit's house to get his car to take the girls home. Two-Bit and Marcia are continuing to get along, and as they walk Ponyboy and Cherry amaze themselves as they divulge insights as confidants.

Cherry shares her philosophy on what separates the two gangs—not only money but passion as well. The Socs lack strong emotions; they are cool almost to the point of not feeling. Ponyboy is amazed, though, at how similar the two gangs really are; they share a "basic sameness." However, Ponyboy does concede that the two groups' emotional responses to life are different: "It's not money, it's feeling—you don't feel anything and we feel too violently."

As the new friends—Pony, Johnny, Two-Bit, Cherry, and Marcia—walk, a blue Mustang passes, a car that the girls identify as belonging to their boyfriends, Randy and Bob.

After a moment of tenseness, the car continues on its way and the group continues their walk. Ponyboy and Cherry resume talking and Cherry asks Ponyboy about Darry. Ponyboy unexpectedly explodes. He complains bitterly about Darry and concludes that he knows that Darry does not like him. Two-Bit and Johnny are stunned. They cannot believe that Ponyboy has made this statement, much less that he believes it. They defend Darry, which only infuriates Ponyboy, so he verbally attacks Johnny about his own terrible home life. In response to this attack, Two-Bit slaps Ponyboy on the side of the head, which sets off a tirade from Ponyboy about the injustice in their world.

The blue Mustang returns and this time it stops. Two Socs get out, and Ponyboy notices that one of them is wearing three heavy rings. Ponyboy puts the blue Mustang together with the rings and realizes that this is the group that had attacked Johnny. Johnny stands terrified. A fight is threatened, but Cherry puts a stop to it, and the girls leave with the Socs.

Two-Bit heads off to hunt up a poker game and maybe to get drunk, and Johnny and Ponyboy decide to lay down in an empty lot and watch the stars. Ponyboy's curfew is midnight, but he assumes that he has plenty of time to make it home. After a rambling fantasy of Ponyboy's—in which he visualizes the perfect life in the country, free of gangs and with his parents still alive—the boys drift off to sleep.

Johnny awakens and sends Ponyboy home, whereupon Ponyboy discovers that it is 2 a.m. Darry has been waiting up for him and is furious. In the heat of the moment, Darry slaps Ponyboy and instantly regrets it. Ponyboy now knows for sure that Darry doesn't want him and runs out the door followed by Darry's cries of regret.

Pony heads back to the vacant lot, wakes Johnny, and announces that it is time for them to run away. Johnny tries to calm Ponyboy. Johnny points out that Ponyboy is lucky to have family who cares about him, and that the gang members never really take the place of family in Johnny's life. They walk to the park, and Ponyboy decides to return home after cooling off a bit.

Commentary

Character
Insight

Ponyboy's character grows as his perspective changes, and he realizes the many similarities that he and Cherry share. Cherry asks whether he watches sunsets, and Ponyboy answers that he does. She admits that she enjoys watching them, but that she hasn't had much time for it lately. A sunset, which they both can watch from their respective homes, represents their outlooks on life.

To Cherry, a sunset is the fading of daylight, when the sun drops below the horizon. It takes away a day and signals the beginning of another, a fresh start. Cherry has, at this point, apparently given up and accepted the rat race: "We're always going and going and going, and never asking where." She also accepts that she is a Soc ". . . if I see you in the hall at school or someplace and don't say hi, well, it's not personal or anything."

To Pony the sunset signals that everyone now is in the dark, one cannot escape the sunset no matter how rich or poor they may be. It is the great equalizer, and it gives everyone a second chance. Ponyboy realizes that "maybe the two different worlds we lived in weren't so different. We saw the same sunset."

Ponyboy and his gang are not the only outsiders; Cherry is an outsider as well. She feels trapped in her world and from her perspective can only see Ponyboy and his friends as unattainable, a realization that saddens her. Her comments about Dally justify her irrational admiration for him: "I could fall in love with Dallas Winston . . . I hope I never see him again, or I will."

Ponyboy's fellow gang members internalize differently the premise that life isn't fair. However, Two-Bit appears to accept his place in life good-naturedly. "Like it or lump it" is his philosophy. On the other hand, Johnny, having been pushed to the brink, vents his frustration and foreshadows his future when he says, "I can't take much more."

At this point, Ponyboy's character is the only one that the reader can actually perceive to be growing in understanding. But readers must remember that Ponyboy is narrating this tale; *his* views are being related.

Often, a literary work that is narrated by one of the main characters creates limitations in terms of the readers' ability to objectively analyze other characters. The story is being told by only one character, and, obviously, readers empathize with that character's outlook.

This chapter reveals that Ponyboy's parents were killed only eight months previously, an important element concerning the concept of family in the novel. Ponyboy is probably still working through the stages of grief. He is filled with anger over losing his parents, which in itself is an important component in his internalization of the unfairness of his life.

After the death of this parents, his life turned from a stable existence to a series of uncertainties, especially with the threat of the authorities revoking Darry's guardianship and splitting up the brothers always looming over his head. Ponyboy is undoubtedly very unstable at this point in his life. One slap from Darry could easily make him overreact.

The power of *three* again asserts its strength in this chapter, but note that this theme applies not only to the greasers but to the Socs as well.

For example, when the Socs stop Ponyboy, Johnny, and Two-Bit on the way home from the movie with Cherry and Marcia, the three rings on the Soc's hand send Johnny over the edge: "Johnny was breathing heavily and I noticed he was staring at the Soc's hand. He was wearing three heavy rings." These were the rings that enabled the Soc to severely beat Johnny and thereby turn his life a different direction.

However, the three greasers—Two-Bit, Ponyboy, and Johnny—were able to stand together against the Socs and use their number to avoid a confrontation.

This chapter concludes with a statement by Ponyboy that foreshadows impending doom: "Things gotta get better, I figured. They couldn't get worse. I was wrong." The reader has already been introduced to a group of possible villains, Johnny's attackers, and this sentence opens up a world of possibilities. Readers begin to feel the insecurity that the constant threat of violence instills in the novel's characters.

Literary Device

Hinton employs the use of a tease sentence very effectively throughout the book. Readers are compelled to go on to the next chapter to find out what happens, and they are engaged in trying to guess the next turn in the plot.

Glossary

buckskin a yellowish-gray horse.

ornery **1** having an ugly or mean disposition **2** obstinate.

quarter short for "quarter horse," any of a breed of light, muscular horse of a solid, usually dark color: because of its quick reactions, it is much used in Western range work and in rodeos.

soused [Slang] intoxicated.

snooker a variety of the game of pool played with fifteen red balls and six other balls.

cur a dog of mixed breed; mongrel.

Chapter 4

Summary

Ponyboy and Johnny reach the park around 2:30 a.m. A blast from a car horn alerts them that the blue Mustang is near. The boys realize that they are outnumbered as five Socs climb out of the car, including Bob and Randy, Cherry's and Marcia's boyfriends. These Socs had threatened Two-Bit, Johnny, and Ponyboy earlier in the evening when they found them walking with Cherry and Marcia. Johnny pulls his switchblade, but a weaponless Pony is grabbed before he knows it and shoved face first into a chilling fountain. In fear, Pony gasps for air but realizes too late that he is sucking in water and drowning.

Ponyboy awakens on the pavement gasping for air. Johnny is next to him and tells him, "I've killed that boy." Johnny is stained with blood and is still clutching his switchblade. Ponyboy sees the Soc, Bob, lying in a pool of blood. Johnny is cool, as Ponyboy has never before seen him, and states that they need money, a gun, and a plan. Knowing that Dally is the gang member with the resources to help them, they go in search of him to a party at the home of Buck Merril, Dally's rodeo partner. They find Dally there, and he provides them with $50, a gun, warm, dry clothes for Pony, and a plan that includes a safe hiding place. Dally instructs them to hop a train to Windrixville, hike up Jay Mountain, and stay in an abandoned church until he comes for them.

Ponyboy and Johnny follow Dally's instructions. On their walk up the mountain to the church, they notice that their appearances contrast sharply with the country culture. The church gives Ponyboy a creepy feeling, perhaps a premonition, but sleep overtakes both boys and any fears or premonitions are lost to exhaustion.

Commentary

Character Insight

Chapter 4 contains one of the novel's primary climaxes, the decisive turning point to which many of the preceding chapters' foreshadowing alludes. When he kills Bob, Johnny loses the look of a wild animal caught in a trap and instead he "looked as cool as Darry ever had." By killing Bob, Johnny takes control of his life in the only way that he thinks is possible. This single action starts a series of events that leads Ponyboy on a path of self-examination, characterized by his statement, "There are things worse than being a greaser."

Ponyboy blames Darry for starting this string of events just as many children—and adults—blame their parents for all of their misfortunes. As a result of frustration and fear for Pony's safety, Darry had slapped him when he returned home well after curfew. This slap did make Pony run away, thus in Ponyboy's mind starting this whole nightmare: "I bet Darry's sorry he ever hit me."

When Johnny and Ponyboy turn to Dally for help, Dally reacts to Ponyboy the same way that Darry did, questioning Ponyboy's common sense. It is ironic that as Pony turns his back on Darry, another person steps in to question his judgment, and thereby prompts Pony to see Dally's perspective, and maybe Darry's, of himself.

The belief that one's parents are responsible for their children's misfortunes does not enter into Johnny's rationale for his actions. Johnny's abusive parents could easily have been blamed for their son murdering another person, but that thought doesn't occur to Johnny. His thoughts are self-motivated. Recall that in the previous chapter, Johnny said, "I can't take much more." This quote highlights Johnny's taking responsibility for his own actions. He doesn't blame his parents for making him live on the street, perhaps placing him in situations where trouble could occur. He accepts his fate, and decides to change it. This contrasts with Ponyboy not acknowledging that his own irresponsibility may have led to this situation.

The fantasy of life in the country hits Pony square in the face as he and Johnny hop off the freight train. The boys' appearance contrasts sharply with the natural beauty around them: "The dawn was coming. It was lightening the sky in the east and a ray of gold touched the hills. The clouds were pink and meadow larks were singing." They realize that their much struggled for "look," a style that guaranteed them the ability to fit in, now works against them. Johnny, with his black T-shirt, blue jeans, and greased long hair, and Pony, with his worn jeans and Dally's leather jacket, realize that "They'll know we're hoods the minute they see us." Both boys know they need to shed that applied appearance to match the culture around them because once again they are outsiders.

Theme

Colors play an important role in this chapter. Johnny is white with fright, "white as a ghost." White contains all of the visible rays of the color spectrum. It is a crossover color that cannot be affiliated with anyone. It combines all colors, and therefore is not a greaser or a Soc color. The color white can be used to describe any character, thus allowing readers to recognize that there are similarities between the two gangs. Some things, such as fright, are universal.

That life is easier and better for others than for themselves is easy for Johnny and Ponyboy to believe. The Socs' lives had appeared to be better than theirs, and now the country life appears wonderful with gold-touched hills and meadowlarks singing.

Glossary

pickled [Slang] intoxicated; drunk.

Hank Williams (born *Hiram Williams*) (1923–53) U.S. country music singer and composer.

corn-poney [Slang] unsophisticated, cornball.

premonition 1 a warning in advance; a forewarning **2** a feeling that something, especially something bad, will happen; foreboding; presentiment.

Chapter 5

Summary

Waking up in a church with the dull realization that Johnny's killing of Bob and the flight from the law really did happen, Ponyboy daydreams about being with Darry and Soda and how wonderful life was at home. Johnny had gone for supplies and returned with food, cigarettes, soap, peroxide, a deck of playing cards, and the book *Gone with the Wind*. In an effort to blend in and disguise their appearances, Johnny cuts and bleaches Ponyboy's hair; Ponyboy in turn cuts Johnny's hair. Following Dally's orders, they stay inside the church and pass the time playing poker and reading aloud from *Gone with the Wind*. This routine continues for five days until Dally shows up and brings them back in touch with the outside world.

Dally brings news, and a letter for Ponyboy from Sodapop. Soda had discovered Pony's sweatshirt at Buck's and realized that Dally knew where Pony was hiding. Soda's letter expresses how worried both he and Darry are and how much they miss Pony.

Dally had been picked up and questioned about the murder, and had let it slip that the boys might be heading for Texas. Because of this misinformation, Dally tells Johnny and Ponyboy that it is safe to go out for a drive and get some food. They head down the mountain with Dally at the wheel doing 85 miles per hour. They stop at a Dairy Queen and both boys eat nonstop. While Johnny and Ponyboy inhale many rounds of food, Dally gives them a quick rundown of the events back home. Because of the killing, the Socs and the greasers are engaged in all-out warfare, and a major rumble is planned. The greasers have a secret weapon; they have a spy working for them: Cherry Valance.

Commentary

The cutting of Ponyboy's and Johnny's hair is a very symbolic gesture. On the surface, their new short haircuts offer them a disguise, but the haircuts also exemplify the fact that they are cutting their ties with the past. They are no longer greasers; unfortunately, they are now fugitives. By losing their hair, the outward trademark of their identity, they change perspectives—not only from their own point of view, but the perspectives of others around them. Dally is the first to see the transformation: "He looks different with his hair like that."

Pony's hair was his pride and joy; now, not only does he lose it, but he also changes its color. His hair color changes from a reddish hue— a warm, comfortable color—to white. White contains all the colors of the spectrum and is a crossover color that cannot be affiliated with anyone. As in earlier chapters, the color white brands him as an outsider— this time to his own identity as a greaser.

Cutting their hair forces the boys to deal with the trauma of their situation. After crying and venting their emotions, they settle into life in hiding at the church. To help pass the time, they read *Gone with the Wind*. The Civil War novel begins to take on special significance in this story. Johnny, especially, likes the book, and Pony is amazed that Johnny can get more meaning out of the story than he can. Johnny didn't do well in school: "—he couldn't grasp anything that was shoved at him too fast, and I guess his teachers thought he was just plain dumb. But he wasn't. He was just a little slow to get things, and he liked to explore things once he did get them."

Johnny's love for the book—and his ability to get more meaning out of this novel than Pony does—defies society's assumptions about Johnny and greasers in general, especially with regard to what they can accomplish and enjoy. The class distinction between the greasers and the Socs becomes blurred, indicating that being an outsider is a matter of perspective (a recurring theme in the book).

Johnny is especially impressed with the Southern gentlemen. Johnny relates to these men because they are gallant and cool even when everything is against them, just like the greasers are.

The South had attempted to secede from the union, and at the time of the *Gone with the Wind* story, they were losing the Civil War. They were the "outsiders" and in the novel they are gallant even in the face of defeat.

Johnny says "I bet they were cool guys" when he learns that the Southern gentlemen rode into sure death because they were gallant. He says of them "They remind me of Dally." And he tells Ponyboy a story about Dally getting picked up by the police (for a crime that Two-Bit actually committed) and staying cool and calm throughout the ordeal, just like the Southern gentlemen. Ponyboy begins to understand Johnny's hero worship of Dally. Ponyboy likes his escapes from life—his books, clouds, and sunsets—but Dally isn't like the heroes in Pony's books; Johnny worships him because he is frighteningly real.

Theme

The colors of the countryside continue to comfort the boys. Ponyboy's appreciation of these colors—"I loved to look at the colors of the fields and the soft shadings of the horizon"—helps temper his view of the world. Ponyboy better understands that he lives not in a black and white world, a world that is either greaser or Soc exclusively, but in a world with many layers in between these two extremes. The colors of the countryside help Pony with this realization. In the city, he was on the same path to understanding, drawn to the beauty of sunsets. Speaking to Ponyboy, Johnny admits, "I never noticed colors and clouds and stuff until you kept reminding me about them."

Character Insight

Ponyboy recites a poem that he has memorized, *Nothing Gold Can Stay*, by Robert Frost. The fact that he has committed this poem to memory is another clue to his character's depth. This poem symbolizes the death of his parents, the goodness of life with them, and the inevitability that all of life will change.

Reciting this poem to Johnny allows Pony to admit that there is still more to understand about not only himself but the world. The colors in the world around him help him see the contrasts present in the world—although sometimes overlooking them is easier. Ponyboy explains, "I liked my books and clouds and sunsets. Dally was so real he scared me." Dally is as real as any sunset, but he is frightening and, therefore, safer for Ponyboy to overlook.

The poem *Nothing Gold Can Stay* creates another bond between Johnny and Ponyboy. Pony confides to Johnny that he couldn't have recited that poem to any of the other gang members, except maybe his brother, Soda. Johnny understands and offers the conclusion that maybe the two of them are just different from the others; Pony disagrees and says that, no, maybe the rest of the gang are the ones who are different.

Ponyboy's family life with Darry and Sodapop, a life that had seemed so unfair to him, seems more perfect now that he is a fugitive and an outsider to the family. He sincerely misses his brothers. Note that his first questions to Dally when Dally arrives are not about his and Johnny's plight but about Soda.

Hinton uses the reflective narration technique to lead the reader in many different directions. She encourages readers to be sympathetic toward the boys because of the conditions in which they are living, but makes clear that Johnny did kill a young man.

In this chapter, Johnny reminds Ponyboy of this fact and the implications of Bob's death. Even though Ponyboy does not want to recognize the consequences of this act, Hinton uses this technique to remind readers to do just that: "Then for the first time since Dally and I had sat down behind those girls at the Nightly Double, I relaxed. We could take whatever was coming now."

And, just when the reader believes that the foreshadowing in previous chapters has led to the worst the characters must endure, Hinton slips in another piece of foreshadowing in the line, ". . . if that old church ever caught fire there'd be no stopping it." Combine this statement with her tease at the end of the chapter—the discovery that Cherry is a spy for the greasers—and the reader is efficiently lured into turning the next page.

Glossary

peroxide hydrogen peroxide, a liquid used to bleach hair.

gallant 1 showy and lively in dress or manner **2** stately; imposing **3** brave and noble; high-spirited and daring.

Robert Frost (1874–1963) U.S. poet.

T-bird [Slang] a Ford Thunderbird.

elude to avoid or escape from by quickness, cunning, and so on; evade.

heater [Slang] a pistol.

Chapter 6

Summary

That Cherry Valance is acting as a spy for the greasers shocks Pony-boy and Johnny, but then they learn that Bob, the dead Soc, had been her boyfriend. Dally informs them that Cherry has said that she is will-ing to testify that the Socs were drunk that night and that Johnny acted only in self-defense. Cherry's stance gives Johnny the hope he needs, and he announces that they are going to turn themselves in to the police. A stunned Dally rejects this plan, but Johnny only maintains, "I don't aim to stay in that church the rest of my life."

Dally relates to the two boys how worried the gang is about them. Johnny just keeps asking whether his parents have been worried. Dally avoids the question as long as he is able, but then has to admit to Johnny that, no, his parents have not asked about him. Johnny doesn't say any-thing, but looks devastated. Driving back from Dairy Queen, they spot the church on fire. A group of people stands around the church; a school evidently out on a picnic, and Ponyboy and Johnny jump out of the car to find out what's happening. As they arrive on the scene, one of the women shouts that some of the children are missing.

Both Ponyboy and Johnny leap through a window in search of the kids. An older man—later identified as Jerry Wood—follows them, but he is unable to get through the small window. The boys quickly find the kids and hand them out through the window to safety. Dally is now on the scene and he warns the boys to get out because the roof is start-ing to cave in. After dropping the last kid out the window, Johnny shoves Pony out the window, and the roof collapses. Pony blacks out, but Dally goes back inside for Johnny.

When Ponyboy regains consciousness, he hears sirens. He assumes that he is in a police car until Jerry Wood (who accompanies him) tells him that they are in an ambulance, and Johnny and Dally are in the ambulance behind them. Dally has a badly burned arm, but Johnny is in far worse condition, with a possible broken back and bad burns. They are all considered heroes for saving the children. At the hospital, doctors examine Ponyboy, and except for a few burns and a big bruise across his back, he's fine. He is in the waiting room, worried about Johnny and Dally, when Darry and Soda arrive. Soda gives Pony a great big bear hug, and Darry stands back with his hands dug into his pockets. When Pony looks at Darry he sees that he is crying. In that split second, Ponyboy realizes that Darry does care for him, that he was just trying too hard. After losing his parents, Darry fears losing another loved one.

Commentary

Cherry's willingness to clue the greasers in on Soc activity shows her to be in a kind of limbo. She is no longer affiliating herself as a Soc, but instead is watching them as an outsider. However, the gang definitely does not consider her to be a greaser, because she is merely reporting to them to prevent any more fights between the rival groups. This existence, not being affiliated with one group or another, can be a scary one. It is especially frightening to adolescents who use the group mentality as a barometer of their own self worth. However, sometimes it is necessary to step outside of one's own comfort zone to stand up for an issue in which you believe. This is what Cherry is doing: Tired of the fighting and the gang mentality, she attempts to resolve the many *perceived* differences that separate the two groups.

This turn in Cherry's personality in some ways more closely aligns her with Dally. Dally is a greaser, but he is the most outcast of the group. He is the only one who has ever been in serious trouble, and he is the only one whom everyone in the group, including Darry, is afraid of: "Not even Darry wanted to tangle with him. He was dangerous," Ponyboy remembered.

Hinton describes Dally's hair as "white"-blond" a good color for someone who could be an outsider from all groups. White contains all of the visible rays of the color spectrum. It is a crossover color that cannot be affiliated with anyone. If Hinton were to write a sequel using Dally and Cherry, it would be easy to draw an analogy between them and Romeo and Juliet. Both couples are teenagers who come from different worlds. Romeo and Juliet deal with feuding families who oppose their relationship, and Dally and Cherry battle opposing gangs.

The perception that the three boys are heroes goes beyond gang lines. (The power of three is a theme that is prevalent throughout Western literature.) Three greasers, whom Bob had defined as "white trash with long hair," seemingly defy all stereotypes and risk their lives to save some children. This is a concept that Ponyboy thought no one could believe. Ponyboy explains the events to Jerry Wood—from the drive-in theatre, to the killing, to their escape—but Wood does not change his perception of the bravery displayed by Johnny, Pony, and Dally. Ponyboy notes of Wood, "He didn't seem to mind our being hoods."

Character Insight

The most important revelation in this chapter is Ponyboy's redefinition of his family. From talking with both Dally and Johnny, Ponyboy realizes how lucky he is to have two brothers—not just gang-member brothers, but two real brothers. Pony internally admits that he loves them both even if they aren't always the way he wants them to be.

He understands that he is lucky compared to Johnny, who relies on the gang to be his brothers and serve as his only family because his parents don't care about him: "Darry and Sodapop were my brothers and I loved both of them, even if Darry did scare me; but not even Soda could take Mom and Dad's place. And they were my real brothers, not just sort of adopted ones."

In the hospital, when Pony, Darry, and Soda reunite, this new appreciation of his brothers is tested. Ponyboy demonstrates no hesitation in showing his love for Soda when he arrives at the hospital, but he initially stands off from Darry. It isn't until Pony sees Darry crying that the love for his brother triggers a moment of enlightenment: "In that second what Soda and Dally and Two-Bit had been trying to tell me came through." Now Pony understands that Darry had been trying too hard in his new role of guardian and protector.

Pony realizes that Darry really does care. Pony is able to go to Darry and hug him, just like he hugged Soda. This love that he feels from and for his brothers makes everything all right. The *three* brothers are united as a family, a source of strength to all of them.

Glossary

JD short for juvenile delinquent.

Chapter 7

Summary

As the three brothers wait at the hospital to find out about their friends' conditions, reporters bombard them with questions. Finally, Darry convinces the reporters to leave, but the nurses still will not give Pony, Soda, and Darry any information about the conditions of Dally and Johnny (medical information is privileged and is only given to family members). Darry manages to convince the doctor that they, the three Curtis brothers, are the only real family that these two boys have, so the doctor gives them the bad news. Dally's one arm is severely burned, but he will eventually regain full use of it. Johnny is in critical condition; his back is broken and he is suffering with third-degree burns. *If* he lives, he will not be able to walk for the rest of his life. The realization that if he lives, he would have to stay in his parents' house, a place he hates, for the rest of his life is too much for the brothers. They decide to go home for the night.

Ponyboy is the first one up the next morning and is making breakfast when Steve and Two-Bit stop by. They tease Ponyboy about being a hero and show him the story about him in the paper. The coverage is very positive for the brothers, and the final line states that the boys should be allowed to stay together. This is the first time Pony realizes that he and Soda might be put in a boys' home. He questions Darry about it, and then confesses to him that he has had another bad nightmare. The nightmares started after their parents were killed and after one nightmare scenario, he always wakes up screaming or in a cold sweat. The worst part is that he can never remember them.

Ponyboy isn't feeling well, but he and Two-Bit leave the house and walk toward the hospital to visit Dally and Johnny. The blue Mustang reappears and eventually pulls over. Ponyboy recognizes Randy Adderson (Marcia's boyfriend) and the tall Soc who had tried to drown him. Pony hates them, it is their fault Bob is dead, Johnny is dying, and he and Soda might be placed in a boys' home.

Randy asks him why he saved those children at the burning church. Randy says that he would never have done it, and that he can't believe that a greaser would do anything like that. Pony explains that it wasn't a greaser or a Soc issue—the decision is dependent on the individual. Randy states that he isn't going to fight in the big rumble that is planned for that night. The fight isn't going to solve anything and no one will really win. As Ponyboy gets out of the car, Randy says, "Thanks, grease . . . I didn't mean that, I meant, thanks, kid." "My name's Ponyboy. . . . Nice talkin' to you, Randy." Ponyboy thinks, "Socs are just guys after all. Things are rough all over, but it was better that way. That way you could tell the other guy was human too."

Commentary

Ponyboy has matured remarkably over these past chapters, and those around him make progress as well. His interaction with Randy, a Soc who is older than he is, paints Pony as the mature one. Note also that those characters who have had interaction with Ponyboy seem to have matured the most. When someone is struggling to understand life, the people around are often drawn into the analysis. Johnny, in particular, changed after spending five days with Pony. His sensitivity and appreciation for the world around him is markedly heightened.

Every family has their own traditions. Honoring these traditions is often done subconsciously. Traditions can give individuals a sense of security and belonging, and the same is true for the Curtis family. Ponyboy knew that the first one up in the morning was responsible for making breakfast. He feels a sense of responsibility to honor this tradition, and cooking breakfast provides him with the security of belonging. However, traditions are not always good. Steve Randle, Soda's best friend and fellow greaser, is experienced in painful traditions. About once a week, his father orders him to move out of the family home. Steve knew that the next day his father would give him five or six dollars to make up for throwing him out, but the cruelty of his father still hurt. The reader learns in this chapter that the murder victim, Bob, also did not have the best of family traditions. On the surface he appeared to have everything, but his parents allowed him to "run wild" all of the time; he was "spoiled rotten." Their tradition was to set no limits for Bob, and, unfortunately, Bob knew this. Bob also knew that his parents accepted the blame for everything that he did. Bob didn't necessarily want this parent/child relationship, in which he never faced responsibility, but he knew that parenting style was the tradition.

Everyone needs some limits set on his or her behaviors and to be held responsible if expectations are not met. For example, Darry sets limits for Pony, and Pony now understands that the limits mean that Darry only wants what is best for him. The consequences for Pony's running away now loom frightfully large on the horizon. For he and Soda to be sent away and the family separated would be tragic for all concerned.

Note that in this chapter the reader is told many times that Ponyboy is not feeling well, or not feeling quite right. He is too tired, takes aspirin for a headache, but still doesn't feel right. These health clues are not really foreshadowing, because Hinton does not directly allude to an outcome. However, readers can learn to anticipate possible story directions. Hinton does not come right out and tell readers that more is going on than what is overtly expressed on the page, but a careful reader will not be surprised by future events.

This chapter also makes the first reference to the nightmares Pony has been suffering from since his parents' death. Dreams have been an element in earlier chapters, and it was in Chapter 3 that a daydream about a perfect life in the country turned into sleep that in turn began the nightmare with Johnny.

In both Chapters 4 and 5, Pony wishes that everything that happened was a dream: "I half convinced myself that I had dreamed everything that had happened the night before." Perhaps his nightmare has returned to coincide with the nightmare that he is dealing with in his waking life. Readers can be drawn deeper into the story by attempting to draw potential outcomes from these clues. Have the nightmares returned because the brothers face a permanent separation? Or, is it foreshadowing the possible loss of Johnny? Again, the ability to read between the lines can add insights into characters and draw the reader deeper into the story.

Glossary

exploit an act remarkable for brilliance or daring; bold deed.

contemptuously in a manner full of contempt; scornfully; disdainfully.

Chapter 8

Summary

When Two-Bit and Ponyboy arrive at the hospital, the nurses won't let them see Johnny. However, the doctor permits their visit because Johnny has been asking for them and it "can't hurt now." With that foreboding statement, the boys go in and find Johnny awake and able to talk. Johnny knows that his condition is not good, and he is afraid of dying. He tells them that 16 years is not enough living and that it is just not fair. Johnny's mother shows up to visit him, but Johnny refuses to see her: "Tell her to leave me alone. For once." He passes out after this incident, and it is evident that he is experiencing a great deal of pain.

Pony and Two-Bit also visit Dally, who is still in the hospital. He is his old self, and resents the fact that he will not be able to take part in the rumble that night. He asks Two-Bit for his black-handled switchblade and, upon receiving it, places it under his pillow.

The boys leave Dally and decide to take the bus home. Two-Bit leaves Pony at the bus stop while he goes into the gas station for cigarettes. Pony has almost fallen asleep when Two-Bit returns, and Two-Bit questions his health. Ponyboy begs him not to tell Darry that he is ill and assures him that as soon as he takes a handful of aspirins he'll be fine and ready to rumble. Two-Bit reluctantly agrees.

Ponyboy has a bad feeling about the rumble. He tries to convey it to Two-Bit, but Two-Bit doesn't want to understand. He accuses Pony of being a chicken, but Pony defends himself and says that it isn't about being chicken, it is about the awful feeling that something bad is going to happen at the rumble.

Cherry Valance is at the vacant lot when the boys go by. She speaks to both Pony and Two-Bit and assures them that the Socs are going to follow the rules—no weapons. Pony asks her whether she is going to visit Johnny in the hospital, but she says that she just can't because Johnny had killed her boyfriend. She doesn't try to defend Bob's actions, but she laments the fact that he is dead.

Pony doesn't want to hear her regret about Bob's death and questions her sincerity in being a spy: "Don't you ever try to give us handouts and then feel high and mighty about it." Pony instantly regrets saying this, thereby slipping back into old greaser habits. He tries to counter that statement by asking her about the sunset, and she realizes his contrition and smiles. As they part he notices that she has green eyes, the same as his.

Commentary

The Outsiders seems to hit all of the hot issues that confront teenagers. This chapter starts out with a diatribe against suicide. Suicide is a critical issue for teens, and Johnny's lack of choice about his living or dying brings him a new perspective. He is angry with himself (for not valuing his life when he had the time) and at life itself (for not being fair): "I used to talk about killing myself . . . I don't want to die now. It ain't long enough."

He regrets not learning more, doing more, and experiencing more. He regrets losing the opportunity of living while he had the chance: "I wouldn't mind it so much if there wasn't so much stuff I ain't done yet and so many thing I ain't seen. It's not fair."

Character Insight

Johnny's perspective regarding his mother also changes. His mother finally comes to the hospital to see him, and he turns her away. Note that his wanting her to leave him alone contrasts sharply with his earlier statement in Chapter 3, when he laments to Ponyboy, "I stay away all night, and nobody notices." And in Chapter 6, when Dally picked Pony and Johnny up at the church in Windrixville, Johnny was upset that his parents hadn't even wondered where he was. Perhaps Johnny's refusal to see his mother when she visits the hospital suggests that he doesn't want to be the victim anymore, or maybe he wants to hurt her emotionally the way she has so often hurt him.

The lines that separate the greasers from the Socs continue to fade. Two-Bit brings up the topic of the impending rumble and asks Pony whether he realizes that if it weren't for their gang, Darry would be a Soc. Here, Two-Bit perhaps unknowingly alludes to the concept that no matter how hard an individual tries to separate himself from who he is, it doesn't work. Perhaps Darry already knew that his affiliation with the greasers was for his brothers' benefit. Or maybe Darry recognized the need for the extended family that his gang offered. After all, the death of his parents only eight months earlier certainly has changed both his and his brothers' lives. If their parents were still alive, they might not need a gang. Darry would have been in college, and Soda would not have dropped out of school.

Ponyboy is still trying to accept the idea that everyone is human. Intellectually he knows that life can be a challenge for everyone, but his conversation with Cherry shows that his heart sometimes speaks first. The concept that "Things are rough all over" is easier to accept in one's head than one's heart. Cherry, sitting in her pretty red Sting Ray, only seems to remind Pony of how unfair life can be. The words out of his mouth ("Don't you ever try to give us handouts and then feel high and mighty about it.") sting both of their ears, and he quickly wishes he could take them back.

The fact that he does try to equalize the situation by mentioning sunsets does show his growth. Pony has developed a more mature understanding of the world and it is evident here. His perspective is now more than just the insiders versus outsiders viewpoint.

The foreshadowing that Hinton includes in this chapter is varied and teases readers into asking many questions. For example, Dally takes Two-Bit's prized switchblade, but what exactly does he intend to use it for? Will he be at the rumble even though he is supposed to be in the hospital? Now Ponyboy appears to be running a fever—what is wrong with him, and when will he be forced to deal with his illness? And what about Ponyboy's gut feeling that something awful is going to happen? Is Hinton foreshadowing something that is going to happen at the rumble?

By using foreshadowing, Hinton builds suspense into the novel and also makes readers feel the vulnerability and insecurity that the characters must live with on a daily basis.

Glossary

groggy shaky or dizzy, as from a blow; sluggish or dull, as from lack of sleep.

doggedly not giving in readily; persistent; stubborn.

booze-hound [Slang] a drunk.

Chapter 9

Summary

The rumble between the greasers and the Socs is set for 7 p.m. that night. Pony slams down five aspirins while no one is looking; he is still successfully hiding his illness. Still apprehensive about the rumble, Pony questions everyone's motivation for the fight: "Soda fought for fun, Steve for hatred, Darry for pride, and Two-Bit for conformity." Pony can only think of one good reason to fight—self-defense.

As the greasers gather together at the vacant lot, Pony compares the other greasers to his own gang. His gang never uses weapons and has never really hurt anyone. Pony realizes that they (his gang) are not hoods, and they don't belong with this group of future convicts. Pony-boy realizes that, unlike these hoods, Darry has the potential to be successful in life. Pony wants to be like Darry. When the Socs gather, Darry steps forward and says, "I'll take on anyone." One Soc steps forward and says hello to him. It is a former buddy, one who is now in college, while Darry has to work for a living. Just as the rumble begins, Dally shows up. Able to fight with only one arm, he announces that a rumble can't happen without him. The Socs lose the rumble because they run first. Everyone in Pony's gang is banged up, but the greasers win and that is all that matters.

Dally grabs Ponyboy and says that they have to quickly go to the hospital because Johnny is dying. Ponyboy isn't feeling very well himself. He is still sick and has been cut and bruised. When they are stopped by the police for speeding, Dally is able to point to Pony and say that he is rushing him to the hospital. The police officer believes him and escorts them the rest of the way.

Dally and Ponyboy make it to the hospital in time. Johnny is dying and is not impressed that the greasers won the rumble: "Useless . . . fighting's no good." He asks to speak to Ponyboy, and, leaning over him, Johnny's last words are "Stay gold, Ponyboy. Stay gold."

When Johnny dies, Dally bolts out of the room and takes off running.

Commentary

In this chapter, Ponyboy questions his identification with the East Side greasers. As the seriousness of life hits him and he is forced to deal with the issue of mortality, he begins to challenge some long-held beliefs.

He calls the rough and dangerous Shepard and Brumley gang members "Young hoods—who would grow up to be old hoods." He had never thought about the issue before, but now he realizes that their behavior—and their lives—will continue to get worse, not better. He tells himself that Darry isn't going to be an old hood, that he is "going to get somewhere." And Pony vows that he will be successful like Darry and leave behind the neighborhood gang life.

Johnny's dying wish for Pony was for him to "Stay gold." Here, gold symbolizes idealism and goodness. Johnny knew that Pony was capable of accomplishing many goals, but most importantly he saw the good life that Pony had with his brothers. He wanted Pony to realize the importance of these gifts, especially having brothers who are truly family, while he still had them.

The perspective of being an outsider has now almost come full circle. Pony is now beginning to view himself and his brothers as outsiders within the East Side greasers. It is important to remember that seeing oneself as an outsider is a matter of perspective. That perspective can shift as a person begins to look at life and life's situations through different eyes.

In this chapter, Pony begins to notice and show concern about the self-destructive behaviors and attitudes of his gang: for example, Two-Bit's excessive drinking and the gang's motivations for fighting ("Soda fought for fun, Steve for hatred, Darry for pride, and Two-Bit for conformity."). Just before the rumble begins, Ponyboy looks around at the Shepard and Brumley gang members and thinks, "We're greasers, but not hoods, and we don't belong with this bunch of future convicts. We could end up just like them." And, again, the readers can see Ponyboy turning away from the gang life and values.

But he also struggles with the values of the world outside of the gang. He does not place value on a world in which the only thing a young person can be proud of is a reputation, especially a reputation for being a hood and having greasy hair: "I don't want to be a hood, but even if I don't steal things and mug people and get boozed up, I'm marked lousy. Why should I be proud of it?"

Theme

Unfortunately, people are often judged by their appearances. And this line of thinking is linked to the "life isn't fair" theme that weaves its way throughout this story. The greasers grow their hair long and grease it down for a hoody look. The Socs, on the other hand, dress nicely and look decent, which, Pony acknowledges, is "why people can't ever think to blame the Socs and are always ready to jump on us."

Pony realizes that appearances are meaningless (". . . half of the hoods I know are pretty decent guys underneath all that grease, and from what I've heard, a lot of Socs are just cold-blooded mean—but people usually go by looks.").

Character Insight

Pony is recognizing the unfairness of the division between the greasers and the Socs, dictated by economically drawn neighborhood lines. At the beginning of the rumble, when Darry faces off against his former football buddy who is a Soc and now in college, Ponyboy thinks, "... they used to be friends, and now they hate each other because one has to work for a living and the other comes from the West Side. They shouldn't hate each other . . . I don't hate the Socs anymore . . . ."

The fact that Pony is attempting to incorporate into his own life the idea that these class divisions and roles are superficial is another factor that demonstrates his continuing character growth. Life *doesn't* always make sense; life *isn't* always fair.

Teachers often explain that fair is a four-letter word, and they discourage its use in their classrooms. All students have different learning abilities, and what may be considered fair for one student would be totally inappropriate for another. The concept that life isn't fair is a very hard one to understand. Numerous self-help books are on the market today that try to explain the concept to frustrated adults. The fact that Pony is attempting to incorporate that concept in his own life is another factor that demonstrates his continuing character growth.

Glossary

conformity the condition or fact of being in harmony or agreement; correspondence; congruity; similarity.

amplifier 1 a person or thing that amplifies **2** *Electronics* a device, especially one with electron tubes or semiconductors, used to increase the strength of an electric signal.

Chapter 10

Summary

After Johnny's death and Dally's departure, Ponyboy wanders through the hospital's halls in a daze. Pony is in denial about Johnny's death, and keeps repeating that he isn't dead. He leaves the hospital and roams the streets until a stranger picks him up and drives him home.

Upon arriving home, Pony tells the rest of the gang about Johnny's death and everyone is silent. The phone rings, and the call is from Dally. He says that he has just robbed a grocery store and he needs someplace to hide out. The gang members agree to meet at the vacant lot.

They race to the lot to the accompaniment of sirens wailing in the streets. Everyone reaches the lot at the same time: Dally, the gang, and the police. As Dally stands in a circle of light under a street lamp, he pulls out his gun. Pony knows that it isn't loaded and he realizes that Dally knows that, but the police don't. Dally wants to die, and he gets his wish. He is gunned down as his gang watches, knowing that Dally always gets what he wants and this time Dally wants to be dead.

As these events are happening, Pony's condition is worsening. He can barely run to the lot and his vision is shifting in and out of focus. Ponyboy collapses at the lot, as his brothers and gang rush to help him.

The next thing Pony remembers is waking up at home. He doesn't remember being in the hospital or being unconscious for three days, but he does remember that both Johnny and Dally are dead. Darry tells him that he has been suffering from exhaustion, shock, and a minor concussion. The concussion came from the rumble when a Soc had kicked him in the head.

Gone with the Wind is lying on the table. Darry tells him that Johnny had instructed the nurse to give the book to Pony. All Pony can think about are the Southern gentlemen who were going off to certain death in the war—just like Dally. Pony vows never to finish the book.

Soda and Darry spend every moment by Pony's bedside. They are as exhausted as Pony. The future for all three is uncertain. Pony has missed a lot of school, he has missed track, and the threat of being placed in a boys' home is still a very real possibility.

Commentary

Dally's death forces readers to take another serious look at themes that are vital to understanding the novel.

One important theme is the evolution of family relationships. In this chapter, Pony is concerned that he may have only called for Soda, not for Darry, while he was sick and barely conscious. Finally, Soda eases his concerns with assurance that he did ask for Darry.

Early in the book, Pony believed that Darry didn't even like him, much less need him as a brother. After the fire at the church, when Pony was reunited with Darry, Pony finally saw Darry for what he really is: a caring brother who loves him, has sacrificed a great deal for him, and has done his best to parent him. Since the killing of Bob, the flight from the law, and other events, Pony has developed greater maturity and a broader perspective. He is now less self-absorbed, and he is upset when he thinks that he may have hurt Darry's feelings by not calling for him.

The issue of who is an insider and who is an outsider is another important theme. How readers and the novel's characters interpret Dally's death is totally dependent on perspective. For example, Ponyboy says, "Two friends of mine had died that night; one a hero, the other a hoodlum." Readers are forced to examine the question, who is the hero and who is the hoodlum?

Johnny did save the children from the burning church, but he would never have been there in the first place if he hadn't been on the run. Did he kill Bob just to save Ponyboy and himself, or was the killing a self-fulfilling prophecy? Approximately four months ago, the Socs had badly beaten Johnny and he had vowed that "He would kill the next person who jumped him." Hinton is careful not to judge Johnny, deciding instead to leave the decision to the readers.

Dally did rob a grocery store and take the police on a chase that ended in his being shot. However, earlier in the book, Dally had risked going to jail himself in order to help Johnny and Pony when they were fleeing from the law. And Dally did save Pony from certain death by pulling him out of the burning church. He also risked personal injury to go in after Johnny, and pulled him out as well. Even the papers considered him a hero. Note, too, that Dally was always Johnny's hero.

Pony is only beginning to sort out his feelings about the gallantry or futility of the deaths of his two friends. He is in denial, and in this chapter, he often reminds himself not to think about Johnny and Dally. This struggle is made clear by his attitude toward the *Gone with the Wind* novel that Johnny has left him: "I didn't want to finish it. I'd never get past the part where the Southern gentlemen go riding into sure death because they are gallant."

When Pony and Johnny were reading the novel while hiding in the church, Johnny had been impressed with the gallantry of the Southern gentlemen as they faced certain death in battle. The Southern gentlemen had reminded Johnny of Dally. Now, Ponyboy pictures the Southern gentlemen looking like both Johnny and Dally. And then he tells himself, "Don't remember. Don't try to decide which one died gallant."

Dally's dying in a circle of light is intensely symbolic. Light is often connected with enlightenment. Dally knew what he wanted after the death of Johnny: He wanted to die. He pulled an unloaded gun in order to force the police to shoot him.

The fact that his gang witnessed the death of their second gang member in one day suggests that perhaps the circle of light was for them. The light allowed them to vividly see Dally's death, giving them the opportunity to think about whether they, too, want to die, as Pony says of Dally, "violent and young and desperate." Johnny believed Dally was the gallant Southern gentleman. And maybe he was; perhaps by his dying, he showed his friends another way to live.

Glossary

stupor a state in which the mind and senses are dulled; partial or complete loss of sensibility, as from the use of a narcotic or from shock.

indignant feeling or expressing anger or scorn, especially at unjust, mean, or ungrateful action or treatment.

Chapter 11

Summary

Pony is confined to bed for a week, still recuperating and trying to remember and understand the events of the past few days. Looking through Soda's old yearbooks to pass the time, he stumbles across a picture of Robert Sheldon. He recognizes the boy, but he needs a moment to realize that this is the Bob whom Johnny killed. He tries to imagine what Bob had been like, and wonders how his parents are handling his death.

Darry tells him that he has a visitor. Pony welcomes into the room Randy Adderson, a Soc. Randy explains that he is visiting because Cherry has heard his name on the bulletin at school and because everyone involved in Bob's killing has to see the judge the next day regarding the death. Randy says that his dad advised him to just tell the truth before the judge. Randy also tells Pony that he regrets his involvement in the fight because it has upset his father. Pony is amazed, because he sees the consequences Randy faces as minimal—Randy's father is rich; he can pay any fine the judge imposes and clear his son of any charges. Ponyboy and his brothers have avoided talking about the upcoming meeting with the judge. This hearing could possibly be the end of their home life together, and nobody wants to accept that possibility.

Pony tells Randy this fear, and Randy advises him to tell the truth. He continues by stating that Pony isn't guilty of any crime and Johnny was the one who wielded the knife. At this pronouncement, Ponyboy erupts, "I had the knife. I killed Bob." Randy is confused but continues to correct Pony and assure him that Johnny killed Bob. Pony repeats, "Johnny is not dead." Darry rescues Randy from this scene and tells him that he must go. Darry explains to Randy that the doctor has said that Ponyboy is still suffering mentally and emotionally and that only time will heal him.

Commentary

Character Insight

A careful reader is not surprised by the turn of events in this chapter. In the previous chapter, Pony stated about Johnny, "He isn't dead, I said to myself. He isn't dead. And this time my dreaming worked." And as this chapter opens, Pony is looking at Bob's picture in the yearbook and says, "I could begin to see the person *we* had killed." Both of these statements allude to Pony's state of mind: Johnny is not dead, and Pony is assuming responsibility for Bob's death. Pony may be thinking that he is equally guilty of killing Bob because he was at the scene. Legally, he could be held partially responsible because he aided and abetted a known criminal when he and Johnny fled the law. Or he may consider himself guilty simply because he is a greaser. Perhaps it is his fate as a greaser to become the convict he was destined to be. Or maybe Pony subconsciously believes that he is the guilty party because Johnny was saving Pony's life when he killed Bob. Whatever the reasoning, Pony is in a state of denial. Denying that Johnny killed Bob and that now Johnny is dead is the only way that Pony is able to deal with the two deaths.

Theme

Pony feels that Randy's concern over letting his father down is ludicrous. Randy's father is rich enough to pay the fine and clear his son's name, so the family won't suffer from Randy's actions. To draw a contrast and to make his point, Pony tells Randy what the possible implications may be for his own family. (Darry could be removed as guardian, and Soda and Pony could be sent to a boys' home.) Although Randy looks worried upon hearing this information, he doesn't fully understand Pony's fear because he knows that Pony isn't responsible: "You didn't do anything. It was your friend Johnny who had the knife." Each boy feels like an outsider as he tries to understand the other's life. However, as readers have seen throughout the book, being an outsider is a matter of perspective. Randy and Pony actually are experiencing similar emotions while they come to terms with the violent events and consequences. Randy feels that his father is a "good guy" and doesn't deserve to go through this disappointment and embarrassment because of him. And Pony believes that his brothers do not deserve to be separated because of his actions.

Glossary

guardian 1 a person who guards, protects, or takes care of another person, property, and so on; custodian **2** a person legally placed in charge of the affairs of a minor or of a person of unsound mind.

Chapter 12

Summary

The hearing with the judge wasn't what Ponyboy had expected. Everyone except Pony was able to tell the judge what had happened that night; Pony is only questioned about his home life. The judge listens to everyone, acquits Pony, and closes the case. But things are not back to normal at home. Pony is having a hard time at school, and he is forgetful and clumsy. Fighting resumes with Darry as he continually has to berate Pony about getting his homework done. Nothing really matters to Pony any more, and getting through each day is a struggle for him.

At lunch one afternoon, Pony, Two-Bit, and Steve walk over to the gas station. Two-Bit and Steve go inside and a carload of Socs drive up and three get out. Pony feels nothing; he isn't scared or mad. The Socs accuse him of being the one that killed Bob Sheldon, and start coming toward him. Pony calmly breaks a bottle and threatens to "split" them if they don't get back into their car: "I've had about all I can take from you guys." The Socs retreat, and Pony picks up the broken glass.

Pony's English teacher assigns a semester theme for him to write, and if he does well on it, he will give him a C for the class even though his work has earned him a failing grade. The topic is to be Pony's choice and the theme is proving to be an overwhelming task for him to accomplish. Darry's constant nagging only results in arguments. When Darry and Pony try to bring Soda into the fight and ask him to choose sides, he runs out of the house.

Pony and Darry chase after him and finally catch him down at the park. Soda explains that he just can't stand it anymore—always being in the middle, always being torn from one side to the other. Neither Darry nor Pony had ever thought about how their fighting was impacting Soda. Soda reminds them that they should be sticking together, not tearing each other apart. All agree that they need to pull together, not apart.

At home that night, Pony cannot make himself work on his theme. He picks up *Gone with the Wind* and a note from Johnny falls out.

Johnny writes that he had figured out what the poem *Nothing Gold Can Stay* really meant. The meaning is that one should not take things for granted, that everyone needs to continue to look at the world as if it is brand new in order to appreciate it. He also writes that Pony still has plenty of time to make something of himself. There is plenty of good in the world, and, most importantly, Pony should tell Dally these ideas as well. Dally really needs to hear them.

It is too late to tell Dally. Suddenly it dawns on Pony that a lot of Dallys live in the world. Someone should tell their side of the story, from their perspective, and then maybe other people wouldn't be so quick to judge. Pony decides that this is his theme topic. But how to start? Pony starts with the opening lines of Chapter 1.

Commentary

The lack of control that Ponyboy feels in his everyday life leads to his denial and depression that surfaces in these final two chapters. At the time of the hearing, Ponyboy thinks that *he* killed the Soc, not Johnny. But the text assures readers that Ponyboy eventually recovers his memory of the true events of the killing: ". . . the doctor was there and he had a long talk with the judge before the hearing. I didn't know what he had do with it then, *but I do now.*" However, even after he recovers from his denial about the events and knows that Johnny killed Bob, Ponyboy remains emotionally shut down and depressed.

Character Insight

Ponyboy loses interest in life. The events that lead up to this break-down are overpowering; the death of both Johnny and Dally in one day was too much. Plus, the earlier deaths of his parents and the insta-bility of his daily life contributed to what he subconsciously perceives as his best route to his survival: shutting down emotionally, merely walking through life without actively participating in it. Unfortunately, he perceives distancing himself from others as the best way to handle this whole affair.

The author hints about how the other gang members are dealing with the violent events. For example, Two-Bit gripes about losing his prize switchblade, only because that loss is easier to take than the loss of another friend. However, at this point, Ponyboy is not able to see beyond himself. The Ponyboy the readers see at the gas station picking up the broken glass is not a hopeless gang member. Even in his emo-tional shutdown, Pony subconsciously knows that the right thing to do is to pick up the broken pieces of glass, just as his subconscious knows that he will eventually have to pick up the broken pieces of his life and continue on.

Dally had been buddies with his two brothers as well, but as Darry said to Pony, "you just don't stop living because you lose someone." Darry's message of "you don't quit" and life goes on is universal, but it can be very hard to accept. In order to meet his own potential, Ponyboy must overcome his depression, take an active role in his life, and pursue his goals. Darry tells Pony, "You're not going to drop out. Listen, with your brains and grades you could get a scholarship, and we could put you through college." In other words, Ponyboy must stop denying the truth.

Theme

The recurring theme of the power of three dominates this chapter. And now this theme intersects with other themes. For example, family love—based on the *three* brothers—is the power that eventually turns Pony's life around. The stress of being the middle child has been overwhelming for Soda. He has been pulled in two directions, supporting Darry and listening to Pony. He announces that he just can't take the strain of taking sides anymore. His ability to see and understand both Darry's and Pony's points of view is what makes his position as mediator painful. He is not an outsider—he is right in the middle of everything. He should not have to choose sides, because they should choose to stick together—the three of them: "We're all we've got left. We ought to be able to stick together against everything."

This appeal for a truce between Darry and Pony makes sense to the brothers: "Sodapop would always be the middleman, but that didn't mean he had to keep getting pulled apart. Instead of Darry and me pulling apart, he'd be pulling us together."

Johnny's last request for Pony to tell Dally about his interpretation of the poem *Nothing Gold Can Stay* motivates Pony to write this book for all of the Dallys of the world. His reasoning is that maybe *three* people would be alive if someone had told their sides of the story: "One week had taken all three of them." Someone needed to give perspective to their three lives, three lives that were very different but remarkably the same: a Soc who was looking for some limits and someone to tell him no, a juvenile delinquent who believed he had nothing else but limits on his life, and a boy who had accepted defeat too early in life.

Character Insight

The novel concludes with its own opening line, "When I stepped out into the bright sunlight from the darkness of the movie house . . ." and that is what happens to Ponyboy in this novel. A movie house is a dark place where life is reflected to passive observers. Ponyboy steps out of this place and into the real world to be an active participant and pursue his potential. The writing of this essay has been a catharsis for him.

The story has also been a roadmap for the readers to trace Ponyboy's growth. Pony was trapped in the darkness of his life; sinking into depression, denial, and, as Darry describes it, a "vacuum." The darkness symbolized his despair, his lack of understanding, and his feeling of being lost. This essay has forced him out of the darkness and into the bright light. He has taken back control of his life and has realized that he is responsible for taking that step and every one that follows it. Pony is no longer watching his life go by, as an outsider watches a movie on the big screen, but he is taking an active role. His development does not just happen, like a light switch being turned on. Pony takes it one day at a time as he relives this week for the reader.

Literary Device

Only once does he break form and address his audience directly, and that is out of anger and frustration. He is struggling with the unfairness in life and undoubtedly, like most people, he will continue to do so. Remaining in the dark may have been easier for Ponyboy—not caring, only existing, until someone or something pushed him over the edge. He could have been just like Dally, Johnny, and Bob—two greasers and one Soc, all three the same and all three dead. But Ponyboy is the one who finds the strength to step into the light from the darkness.

Glossary

Perry Mason a television drama from the 1960s that featured a lawyer by the same name.

CHARACTER ANALYSES

Ponyboy Curtis

Ponyboy Curtis is a 14-year-old boy whose world has been turned upside down. His parents were killed in an automobile accident just eight months before *The Outsiders* story takes place. He lives with his oldest brother, Darry, who is 20 years old and has legal custody of him and his other brother, Sodapop, who is 16.

Darry characterizes Ponyboy as lacking common sense. Pony agrees with this assessment. He readily admits that he is smart at school, but sometimes he just doesn't think. These occasions get Pony into trouble that he could avoid. This is one aspect of his character that readers are able to see evolve throughout the book. Ponyboy learns that his behavior impacts others, and this newly acquired maturity leads to the telling of *The Outsiders* story.

The brothers are greasers, a class term that refers to the young men on the East Side, the poor side of town. They are known for their long, greased hair. The brothers also belong to a small, tightly knit neighborhood gang. Pony explains, "there are just small bunches of friends who stick together, and the warfare is between the social classes." Pony is the youngest member of their gang, and the other gang members represent extended family members to him. He is able to find security in his friendships with them, and they help fill the void created by his parents' deaths.

Ponyboy narrates the novel, and this narration is a catharsis for him. The reader is able to see the changes in Pony's viewpoints as he is dealing with many issues that are common in an adolescent's life. The most powerful issue is that life is not fair. From the deaths of his parents, to the economic conditions that cast them as greasers, to the deaths of his friends, life is not fair to Ponyboy.

During this two-week period, Pony has to weather three deaths—two greasers and one from the rival gang, the Socs. The Socs, short for Socials, are the "West-side rich kids." By realizing that death at a young age is equally unfair for all of them, Pony is able to not only survive, but to justify his own existence. He takes it upon himself to make their deaths mean something.

Darry and Sodapop Curtis

Darry and Sodapop Curtis are Ponyboy's older brothers who, along with being greasers, are adjusting to life on their own. Darry has taken over the responsibility of guardianship, forfeiting college and working to enable the three of them to stay together. Soda, never very good in school, has dropped out at age 16 and is working to help support the family.

Both boys focus on the future of Ponyboy; ensuring his success is the driving force of the family.

Perspective is a very important issue that runs throughout this novel. Being an *outsider* is a matter of perspective. The brothers' relationships are viewed differently according to each other's perspective. Pony resents Darry's constant nagging and discipline. But Darry is imposing these rules out of concern for Pony's well-being. Pony loves Soda and is thankful for him: "Soda always takes up for me." But he is unaware that the strain of being the one in the middle is almost too much for Soda: "'Golly, you two, it's bad enough having to listen to it, but when you start trying to get me to take sides. . . .' Tears welled up in his eyes, 'We're all we've got left.'"

Johnny Cade

Johnny Cade is "the gang's pet." The novel describes Johnny as a "lost puppy" and a "puppy that has been kicked too many times." He is only 16 years old, but has already been beaten down by the cruelty of life. Johnny had been severely beaten by a group of Socs before this story begins. This beating puts him almost over the edge; in fact, the Socs scared him so much that he even carries a switchblade in his pocket. Johnny vows that, "He would kill the next person who jumped him."

His parents abuse him both physically and verbally, and Johnny often opts to go anywhere but home. The theme of family love is clarified by Johnny many times, because his eyes have seen what family love isn't. Ponyboy tells the readers, "If it hadn't been for the gang, Johnny would never have known what love and affection are."

Johnny idolizes gang member Dallas Winston. Dally is living proof that one can survive without parents or family. Johnny needs to follow in the footsteps of someone in his life and Dally, his hero, is the one he chooses.

The relationship between these two boys is very interdependent. Just before Johnny dies, his relationship with Dally is clarified when Dally tells Johnny that he is proud of him: "Johnny's eyes glowed. Dally was proud of him. That was all Johnny had ever wanted." And Dally needs Johnny as much as Johnny needs Dally. Ponyboy realizes this truth after Johnny's death. When he tries to make sense of Dally's reaction to Johnny's death, it dawns on him, "Johnny was the only thing that Dally loved."

Dallas (Dally) Winston

Dally Winston had been in gangs in New York City before joining the greasers. He is Ponyboy's least favorite member of the gang, and Pony considers him, "tougher, colder, meaner."

Johnny and Pony turn to Dally when they need help escaping after Johnny kills Bob. Dally is there for them, giving Pony, literally, the coat off his own back. Through these gestures, the readers are able to genuinely like Dally. His life experiences seem to have chosen the path for him; the person inside of him never has a chance.

Sherri (Cherry) Valance

To Pony, Cherry Valance typifies the perfect Soc girlfriend. And she is, perhaps, until her boyfriend, Bob, is killed. Cherry, a cheerleader, attends the same high school as Ponyboy. She is cute, rich, and stands up for what she believes in.

Through Pony's friendship with Cherry, he begins to see that "things are rough all over." She challenges Pony to see that the Socs are as individually unique as the greasers are, and as troubled. Cherry acts as a spy for the greasers, and in doing so wants not only to help the greasers, but the Socs as well. She wants the fighting to end, and she does whatever is necessary to even the sides and balance the power between the two rival groups.

Bob Sheldon

Bob Sheldon is the Soc who originally beat up Johnny. He is Cherry's boyfriend, and, like Johnny, he is a victim of his own family. Unlike Johnny, his parents do not physically or verbally abuse him; however, they do something equally as harmful: They allow Bob to shirk responsibility for his own actions.

Bob is the rich kid who has never had to work for anything. His parents have given in to him his whole life, and have never set any boundaries for him. "His parents let him run wild" is the way his best friend, Randy, describes him. Pony wonders, "because they loved him too much or too little?" Johnny kills Bob when the Socs attack Johnny and Ponyboy in a park.

Both Bob and Johnny are victims of their own family relationships.

Randy Adderson

Randy Adderson is Bob's best friend; he is a fellow Soc. After Bob's death, Randy stops Pony on the street and tells him that the fighting between the Socs and the greasers is pointless. Randy refuses to fight in the big rumble because "Greasers will still be greasers and Socs will still be Socs."

Out of friendship, Randy comes to visit Pony while he is sick. Randy tells Pony that he regrets ever being involved with any of the violence because of the impact it is having on his father. Randy believes that his father is disappointed in him. Ponyboy can't fully understand Randy's concerns, because Randy didn't kill anyone, or get hurt in the runble, or see his friend shot down by the police. Because his involvement was minimal, Randy's wealthy father could pay any fines imposed and clear his son. But Randy forces Ponyboy to think about the impact his actions are having on his own family.

Jerry Wood

Jerry Wood is the man at the scene of the fire at the church hideout. He accompanies Pony in the ambulance after the fire. Jerry stays with Pony at the hospital until his brothers arrive. Although Ponyboy confides everything to him, Jerry continues to see Pony, Johnny, and Dally as heroes. He judges them on their actions and not on their appearances.

To be seen as a hero, and not as a hood, is a new experience for Pony. After considering Jerry's judgment call, based entirely on conduct, Ponyboy is able to see his brother, Darry, more clearly. At the hospital Darry is crying and Ponyboy realizes that Darry's eyes might sometimes look cold and hard, but his actions toward him are always motivated by love.

CRITICAL ESSAYS

Themes in the Novel

As the title suggests, *The Outsiders* is a theme in itself. Looking at life as an outsider and feeling as though one is being treated as an outsider is a matter of perspective or point of view. Someone who always feels like an outsider may conclude that life is unfair.

Adolescence is a time when teenagers may consider themselves to be adults, but in reality teens are still under the control of others. Parents, teachers, and other authority figures are always telling them how to live their lives. This loss of control inevitably leads to the feeling that life isn't fair. For example, Ponyboy knows that he is not safe walking the streets in his own neighborhood. He could be attacked solely because of the way he is dressed; he feels like an outsider in his own town. His feelings of powerlessness and vulnerability lead him to conclude that life is not fair.

Ponyboy sees injustice on a daily basis. His parents are dead, Darry is forced to work two jobs to support the brothers, Soda has dropped out of school, and the greasers are looked upon as "white trash." He explains that the gang warfare is actually warfare between the economic classes. Because he is from the poor, East Side of town, his place in life is unfairly predetermined.

The evolution of the family relationships is a recurrent theme in the novel. Family relationships are strained during the teen years, but in the Curtis family, the right to stay together as a family is a constant struggle. Since the death of their parents, Darry has assumed the responsibility of guardianship for Pony and Soda, and under that pressure he has aged beyond his years. He no longer views the two boys as siblings, but rather as a responsibility. Darry recognizes Ponyboy's potential and has high expectations for him. Ponyboy complains that Darry is a stricter disciplinarian than his father, but by the end of the book he understands Darry's role: "Darry *is* a good guardian; he makes me study and knows where I am and who I'm with all the time. . . . My father didn't yell at me as much as he does."

Pony struggles with his expectations for Soda. He is self-conscious about the fact that Soda has dropped out of school, and he wants him to finish his education. Soda did not do well in school, did not like school, and is perfectly content to work in a gas station—a job he loves. Soda also believes that he is doing the right thing by helping to support his family. Pony doesn't care about any of those facts; he just wants Soda to go back to school. Gang relationships are included in the theme of family love. Ponyboy's gang members need the support and security that they find in the gang. The home life situations that these boys find themselves in are often abusive. They have turned to the gang for the love and support that should have come from parents.

Johnny is painfully aware of the difference between the gang and a family and through him Pony begins to understand how lucky he is to have caring family members: "I don't know what it was about Johnny— maybe that lost-puppy look and those big scared eyes were what made everyone his big brother. . . . I thought about it for a minute—Darry and Sodapop were my brothers and I loved both of them . . . they were my real brothers, not just sort of adopted ones." Pony's eventual ability to appreciate his family shows his growth.

The third major theme that runs through *The Outsiders* is the use of colors in a black and white world. Adolescents have a tendency to embrace people and events as absolutes. For example, someone or something is either right or wrong; there can be no middle ground. The characters in *The Outsiders* are either Socs or greasers. People are either rich or poor, good or bad. Hinton descriptively uses color throughout the book to define and add depth to the characters in their environments.

Early in the book, she associates warm colors with the Socs and cool colors with the greasers. Warmth usually is equated with inside and cool is associated with outside, and the colors reflect the characters' positions in society: The greasers view the Socs as insiders and themselves as outsiders.

Using many descriptive colors, Hinton paints the greasers as outsiders. In her original descriptions of Ponyboy's gang, she uses cool colors: Ponyboy's eyes are greenish-gray, Darry's eyes "are like two pieces of pale blue-green ice," Dally's eyes are "blue, blazing ice, cold with a hatred," and Two-Bit Mathews has gray eyes.

Dally is the exception to the rule, "His hair was almost white it was so blond." White contains all of the visible rays of the color spectrum. It is a crossover color that cannot be affiliated with anyone or anything, so it is interesting that Dally, who was "tougher than the rest of us— tougher, colder, meaner," was the one with white/blond hair.

White is also used many times throughout the novel to describe fright, "white as a ghost." The color white symbolizes the internalization that there are no absolutes in the world. To realize that people and events may not be purely right or wrong, good or bad, can be frightening. Dally's white hair exemplifies this concept. Dally appears to be the stereotypical hood: cold, hard, and mean. But he is not that extreme persona. Just like the color white contains all the colors of the spectrum, Dally's character covers a broad spectrum. In addition to his cold, mean image, he is Johnny's hero, he is the one who literally gave Pony the coat off his back, he helped to save the children from the fire, and he was a scared boy who reached out to the Curtis brothers when he most needed help at the end of his life.

Throughout the book, Pony matures and grows in his ability to see the full spectrum, to stop dividing the world into black and white, good and bad, insiders and outsiders, greasers and Socs. Pony's fascination with sunsets at the beginning of the book and, later, his appreciation of the countryside around the church hideout ("I loved to look at the colors of the fields and the soft shadings of the horizon") symbolize this development of his character. A sub-theme within this story is the power of three. Three is a cardinal number that is common in American literature and folklore, and to find it as a pivotal theme in this story is not surprising. Americans have grown up with stories such as *Goldilocks and the Three Bears* and *The Three Little Pigs*. The Holy Trinity is a major doctrine of the Christian faith.

The three Curtis brothers working together have the power to save their family. Three greasers working together save the lives of children trapped by fire. And the three rings on the fist of a Soc change Johnny's life forever, and ultimately lead to three deaths: Bob's, Johnny's, and Dally's.

The Movie versus the Book

Sixteen years after a sixteen-year-old wrote this book, Francis Ford Coppola turned this novel into a movie. The book is a coming-of-age novel, but the movie focuses on the characters' loss of innocence. The movie follows the story line very closely. The reader is only told that this story takes place in the southwest, but the movie places it in Tulsa, Oklahoma, in the year 1966. It also changes the conflict from the East Side versus the West side to the northside versus the southside. This minor directional change was probably made due to the relative time proximity to the musical *West Side Story*, which won the best picture Academy Award in 1961. However, as with all movies, character insight that is critical to understanding the story is lost when the format goes from the written word to the screen. Ponyboy is telling us the story, the same as in the book, but the 91-minute film only glosses over many character relationships.

With the exception of Ponyboy, the viewer misses out on knowing most of the novel's characters. Darry and Soda are relatively minor characters in the movie, and the viewer is given little insight into their lives. The same is true for the rest of the gang, even Dally. Dally's death loses much of its impact because viewers aren't able to get to know him. Only the reader is aware of the fact that Dally's gun is unloaded, and the symbolic death of Dally in the spotlight is gone.

Johnny's character is also weaker in the movie than the book. Viewers don't see the growth in his character, because they don't know Johnny. Johnny's appreciation for life at the end of his own is barely noted, but it has great impact on Pony in the novel.

The whole point of the telling of Ponyboy's story is to give meaning to Johnny's death. Johnny had wanted Ponyboy to tell Dally certain truths, and given that Dally is dead, Pony writes this story down for all of the Dallys in the world: "Someone should tell their side of the story, and maybe people would understand then and wouldn't be so quick to judge a boy by the amount of hair oil he wore." The movie and book do begin and end with the same lines, the difference being, only readers understand the meaning behind them.

Has Society Changed?

The Outsiders, written in the mid 1960s, makes the reader wonder how, if at all, the story would be different if it were told today. The novel includes the usual references that date a story, generally related to pop culture—for example, models of cars, movies, and music—but those are incidentals, and do not affect the narrative or the outcome.

The first thing to consider is the way in which the story is told. If the story were written today, the author probably would continue to use the first-person narrative, because it is a very effective tool for allowing the reader inside the storyteller's mind. The language would be the same, but it would undoubtedly be heavily laced with expletives. The use of swear words, especially by teenagers, is a show of power and a part of everyday life today. The tolerance level for swearing is at a much higher level than it was in the 1960s; current movies and music demonstrate that shift.

Many of the issues that adolescents in the novel face are still very prevalent today. Teenage suicide, pregnancy, smoking, drinking, and the importance of staying in school are still areas of concern for teens. Perhaps the only area that is missing is illegal drug use. Today, undoubtedly, at least one gang member would be using an illegal drug.

Gangs continue to be a part of our society. Gang initiation is not a topic in *The Outsiders,* but perhaps today it would be. Gang initiation in the past was something that happened to the prospective member. Today that prospective member is expected to do something to somebody else or something else. The characters in the novel talk little about acquiring new members, because Ponyboy's gang is like family.

Weapons would be more prominent in a contemporary book than in the 1960's version. The prevalence of automatic weapons and the relative ease in acquiring them would definitely make both the greasers and the Socs more dangerous.

Sex is not addressed in the novel, with the exception of when Soda's girlfriend has to leave town. S. E. Hinton was only sixteen when she wrote *The Outsiders*, and presumably she didn't include sex in the novel because her experiences writing as a teenage boy were limited. In today's more open society, the novel would probably include more discussion of this critical issue for teens. A movie made today would definitely cover this issue.

The premise of the whether the authorities will allow the three Curtis brothers to remain together is still viable. The novel makes reference to the need for a clean, respectable house for the imminent visits of social workers. The same procedure would probably be followed today if the boys had no other living relatives.

Perhaps the scariest change would be in the way the adults and the adolescents relate. On the whole, the teens in *The Outsiders* have little or nothing to do with adults. The few times they cross paths, however, the adults are there to help them. When Johnny and Pony are in the country, and Pony stops a local farmer to ask for directions, he answers the questions kindly and without suspicion, and then laughs, "Boys will be boys."

After Johnny's death, Pony leaves the hospital dazed and confused. A man picks him up, and takes him home to his waiting brothers. Today teenagers often frighten adults—especially teenagers who appear to be gang members. Adults assume that a teen who looks like a hood probably has a gun and will use it. Therefore, an adult is usually not going to stop and help a suspicious-looking teen. Teenagers in the l960s knew that whether they wanted help or not, an adult was usually someone they could turn to in a time of need. That is not the case today. Teenagers are usually on their own—truly outsiders.

CliffsNotes Review

Review Questions

Use this CliffsNotes Review to test your understanding of the original text, and reinforce what you've learned in this book. After you work through the review questions, question and answer section, identify the quote section, and the fun and useful practice projects, you're well on your way to understanding a comprehensive and meaningful interpretation of *The Outsiders*.

1. *The Outsiders* takes place in Tulsa, Oklahoma, during the 1960s. What are the demographics of Tulsa during this time period? Why did Hinton choose this locale? There are no minorities in this story. Did Tulsa have a substantial minority population at that time, and, if so, what ethnic background were they? Why do you think that Hinton did not include any minorities in this story?

2. In 1961, *West Side Story* won the Academy Award for Best Picture. This movie is also about gangs. Hinton would have been 11 years old when the movie first came out, and she wrote *The Outsiders* five years later. Do you think that she was influenced by the movie? How? Are these two stories similar? Are they different?

3. Ponyboy likes to go to movies to escape the reality of his own life. If you were to choose a movie that best gives you the opportunity to escape your own life, what movie would you select and why?

4. The timeline of this story has several inconsistencies. For example, the brothers' parents passed away eight months prior to the beginning of this novel. Hinton states that Darry is 20 years old and has missed out on college because of his responsibility to his brothers. Eight months ago would have possibly made Darry 19, but he should have already started college by that time. Also, the text isn't clear about when the boys joined the greasers. Write a page theorizing when the brothers became greasers and why. If their parents were so wonderful, why did they need a gang?

5. Darry assumes guardianship over his brothers in this story. What does that really mean? They live on their own, so what expenses would the boys have to be responsible for? Write a budget, using today's prices, showing what living on your own would cost for you and your siblings (if you have any). Could you do it? What other expenses are never mentioned? A car? Anything else?

6. The lament that life isn't fair is a major theme in this story. Pick one topic that Ponyboy sincerely feels is unfair and write about the relationship it has with your own life. For example, the fact that Ponyboy's parents were killed in an automobile accident is unfair. Have you ever suffered a family loss that you consider unfair? Choose any topic from the book and write at least one page.

7. Pony and Johnny read from the book, *Gone with the Wind,* while they are hiding out, and Johnny asks for it while he is in the hospital. Upon his death, he gives the book to Pony. What is the significance of this book? Why did Hinton choose this novel and how are the story lines similar?

8. Dally and Cherry are the Romeo and Juliet of this story. Why are they drawn to each other, and if they had gotten together, would their ending have been as tragic as Romeo's and Juliet's in Shakespeare's play?

9. When Pony returns to school after Johnny's and Dally's death, he is unable to function at the level he did before. His grades drop, he's clumsy, and nothing is easy for him. Why does this change occur? Is it a permanent change? How do we know?

Q&A

1. The greasers and the Socs are divided by one factor. What is it?

a. race

b. economics

c. age

2. The greasers' one rule, besides "stick together," is "don't get caught." Why was that rule doubly important for the Curtis brothers?

a. They needed to be on their best behavior to stay together.

b. They had been in too much trouble already.

c. Their father had been a police officer.

3. Ponyboy had never been hit by a member of his family when Darry slapped him for being out so late. What does this slap symbolize?

a. Ponyboy's wake up to a cold, hard reality

b. the unfair treatment he received from his brothers

c. that violence is everywhere

4. Hoppping off the train in the country was like a dream come true for Ponyboy, why?

a. because now they were safe from the law

b. because now he is home

c. because he had dreamed of a perfect life in the country

5. What book kept Ponyboy and Johnny occupied while hiding out?

a. *Great Expectations*

b. *Gone with the Wind*

c. the poetry of Robert Frost

6. What was foreshadowed when the boys stated that they were careful with their cigarettes in the old church?

a. Someone discovered them in the church.

b. They ran out of cigarettes.

c. The fire consumed the church.

7. How did Hinton tip off readers that Dally was going to make it to the rumble?

a. Dally took Two-Bit's knife.

b. Dally and Tim Shepard continued to fight.

c. Johnny encouraged him to go.

8. Why was it important that Johnny died after the rumble?

a. so Johnny could know who won the rumble

b. to show how unimportant the rumble really was—to put it in perspective

c. so Dally and Johnny could visit Johnny again

9. Why did Ponyboy write his theme?

   a. to help himself understand

   b. for his English teacher

   c. for all of the Dally's in the world

   d. all of the above

Answers: (1) b. (2) a. (3) a. (4) c. (5) b. (6) c. (7) a. (8) b. (9) d.

Identify the Quote

1. "In New York, Dally blew off steam in gang fights, but here, organized gangs are rarities—there are just small bunches of friends who stick together, and the warfare is between the social classes."

2. "It seemed funny to me that the sunset she saw from her patio and the one I saw from the back steps was the same one. Maybe the two different worlds we lived in weren't so different. We saw the same sunset."

3. "Shoot," I said, startled out of my misery, "you got the whole gang. . . ." "It ain't the same as having your own folks care about you. . . . It just ain't the same."

4. "That was his silent fear then—of losing another person he loved. I remembered how close he and Dad had been and I wondered how I could ever have thought him hard and unfeeling. I listened to his heart pounding through his T-Shirt and knew everything was going to be okay now."

5. "We're all we got left. We ought to be able to stick together against everything. If we don't have each other, we don't have anything."

6. "I could see boys going down under street lights because they were mean and tough and hated the world, and it was too late to tell them that there was still good in it, and they wouldn't believe you if you did. . . . There should be some help, someone should tell them before it was too late. Someone should tell their side of the story. . . ."

Answers: (1) Ponyboy explains the two gangs, the greasers and the Socs. (2) Ponyboy talks about Cherry Valance, the Soc he met at the drive-in. This statement signals the beginning of his character's growth. (3) Ponyboy and Johnny discuss the difference between a real family and their gang. Johnny understands that the gang relationship is not the same as family, and tries to explain it to Ponyboy. (4) Ponyboy understands the dynamics of his relationship with his brother, Darry. (5) Sodapop is frustrated with his two brothers bickering and tries to pull them all together. (6) Ponyboy realizes that he needs to devote his homework theme—which becomes *The Outsiders* novel— to telling the greasers' story.

Practice Projects

1. Rewrite the end of this story with Johnny surviving. What changes would his living have brought about in the other characters? For example, would Dally still be alive?

2. Create a role-playing game. Make two decks of cards. One deck displays characters—Ponyboy, Darry, and so on—and the other deck reflects situations—both from the book and made-up. Two class members at a time draw from the character pile and together choose a situation. As they create the scene, the rest of the class must identify the characters and discuss the particulars of the scene.

CliffsNotes Resource Center

The learning doesn't need to stop here. CliffsNotes Resource Center shows you the best of the best—links to the best information in print and online about the author and/or related works. And don't think that this is all we've prepared for you; we've put all kinds of pertinent information at www.cliffsnotes.com.

Look for all the terrific resources at your favorite bookstore or local library and on the Internet. When you're online, make your first stop www.cliffsnotes.com, where you can find more incredibly useful information about *The Outsiders*.

Books

This CliffsNotes book provides a meaningful interpretation of *The Outsiders* published by IDG Books Worldwide, Inc. If you are looking for information about the author and/or related works, check out these other publications:

Authors and Artists for Young Adults, is a collection of biographical information about authors and illustrators. Volume 2, Gale Research Inc., 1989.

Meet the Authors: 25 Writers of Upper Elementary and Middle School Books Talk about Their Work, edited by Deborah Kovacs, is a Scholastic Reference Library book that contains articles in which authors discuss their books. Scholastic Trade, 1996.

Presenting S. E. Hinton, by Jay Daly, is a biographical article on the author of The Outsiders. Boston: Twayne Author Series, 1989.

Something About the Author, edited by Anne Commire, offers facts and pictures about authors and illustrators of books for young people. Volume 58, Gale Research Inc., 1990.

Hinton's Works

The Puppy Sister. Jacqueline Rogers (Illustrator). Nick and his parents get more than they wanted when their newly adopted puppy decides to become human. Reprint Edition, New York: Bantam Books, 1997.

Big David, Little David. Alan Daniel (Illustrator). A little boy and his father engage in a battle of wits. New York: Doubleday, 1995.

Taming the Star Runner. A misguided youth, Travis, is sent to live with his uncle and develops an unusual friendship with a young horse trainer. New York: Delacorte, 1988.

Tex. The love between two teenage brothers helps balance the boys parentless life. New York: Delacorte, 1980.

Rumble Fish. A junior high student, Rusty James, usually counts on his big brother, Motorcycle Boy, to come to his rescue, but one day that doesn't happen. New York: Delacorte, 1975.

That Was Then, This Is Now. Two best friends, Bryon and Mark, grow up and grow apart. Viking, 1971.

The Outsiders. The story of Ponyboy, a 14-year-old boy caught up in gang and class rivalry and the tragic consequences. Viking, 1967.

It's easy to find books published by IDG Books Worldwide, Inc. You can find them in your favorite bookstores (on the Internet and at a store near you). We also have three Web sites that you can use to read about all the books we publish:

- www.cliffsnotes.com

- www.dummies.com

- www.idgbooks.com

Internet

Check out these Web resources for more information about S. E. Hinton and *The Outsiders*:

Children's Authors, falcon.jmu.edu/~ramseyil/hinton.htm—This page is a reprint of an interview with S. E. Hinton about why she wrote the novel, Tex.

Mona Kerby's The Author Corner, www.carr.lib.md.us/mae/hint-inf.htm—Mona Kerby is an assistant professor at Western Maryland College. This Web site offers information on a variety of authors and illustrators of young adult books.

Random House, www.randomhouse.com—This site offers descriptions and information about books published by Random House.

Valencia Community College West Campus LRC, valencia.cc.fl.us/lrcwest/hinton.html—The West Campus Learning Resource Center at Valencia Community College in Orlando, Florida, presents this Web site. Their author pathfinders guides include information on over 600 individual authors.

Magazines and Journals

For more information on S. E. Hinton or *The Outsiders*, check out the following journal and magazine articles:

Hinton, S. E. S. E. Hinton: "On Writing and Tex" in Notes from Delacorte Press for Books for Young Readers, Winter, 1979/Spring 1980, 3–4.

"A Book, a Place, a Time: Using Young Adult Novels in a Reading Workshop." English Journal, Volume 84, Number 5, 115–19, 1995.

"Doing Theory: Words about 'The Outsiders.'" English Journal, Volume 81, Number 7, 57–61.

Foster, Herold. "Film and the Young Adult Classic." English Journal, Volume 21, Number 3, 9–13, Spring 1994.

Tighe, Mary Ann and Charles Avinger. "Teaching Tomorrow." ALAN Review, Volume 21, Number 3, 14–17, Spring, 1994.

"Is the Young Adult Novel Dead?" Society of Children's Book Writers and Illustrators, November/December, 1987.

"Face to Face with a Teen-Age Novelist." Seventeen, October, 1967.

"Teen Agers Are for Real." New York Times Book Review, August 27, 1967.

Send Us Your Favorite Tips

In your quest for learning, have you ever experienced that sublime moment when you figure out a trick that saves time or trouble? Perhaps you realized that you were taking ten steps to accomplish something that could have taken two, or you found a little-known workaround that gets great results. If you've discovered a useful tip that helped you understand *The Outsiders* or other books and you'd like to share it, the CliffsNotes staff would love to hear from you. Go to our Web site at www.cliffsnotes.com and click the Talk to Us button.

If we select your tip, we may publish it as part of CliffsNote-A-Day, our exciting, free e-mail newsletter. To find out more or to subscribe to a newsletter, go to www.cliffsnotes.com on the Web.

Index

NOTES

NOTES

NOTES

NOTES

NOTES

NOTES

CliffsNotes

LITERATURE NOTES

Absalom, Absalom!
The Aeneid
Agamemnon
Alice in Wonderland
All the King's Men
All the Pretty Horses
All Quiet on the Western Front
All's Well & Merry Wives
American Poets of the 20th Century
American Tragedy
Animal Farm
Anna Karenina
Anthem
Antony and Cleopatra
Aristotle's Ethics
As I Lay Dying
The Assistant
As You Like It
Atlas Shrugged
Autobiography of Ben Franklin
Autobiography of Malcolm X
The Awakening
Babbit
Bartleby & Benito Cereno
The Bean Trees
The Bear
The Bell Jar
Beloved
Beowulf
The Bible
Billy Budd & Typee
Black Boy
Black Like Me
Bleak House
Bless Me, Ultima
The Bluest Eye & Sula
Brave New World
The Brothers Karamazov

The Call of the Wild & White Fang
Candide
The Canterbury Tales
Catch-22
Catcher in the Rye
The Chosen
The Color Purple
Comedy of Errors…
Connecticut Yankee
The Contender
The Count of Monte Cristo
Crime and Punishment
The Crucible
Cry, the Beloved Country
Cyrano de Bergerac
Daisy Miller & Turn…Screw
David Copperfield
Death of a Salesman
The Deerslayer
Diary of Anne Frank
Divine Comedy-I. Inferno
Divine Comedy-II. Purgatorio
Divine Comedy-III. Paradiso
Doctor Faustus
Dr. Jekyll and Mr. Hyde
Don Juan
Don Quixote
Dracula
Electra & Medea
Emerson's Essays
Emily Dickinson Poems
Emma
Ethan Frome
The Faerie Queene
Fahrenheit 451
Far from the Madding Crowd
A Farewell to Arms
Farewell to Manzanar
Fathers and Sons
Faulkner's Short Stories

Faust Pt. I & Pt. II
The Federalist
Flowers for Algernon
For Whom the Bell Tolls
The Fountainhead
Frankenstein
The French Lieutenant's Woman
The Giver
Glass Menagerie & Streetcar
Go Down, Moses
The Good Earth
The Grapes of Wrath
Great Expectations
The Great Gatsby
Greek Classics
Gulliver's Travels
Hamlet
The Handmaid's Tale
Hard Times
Heart of Darkness & Secret Sharer
Hemingway's Short Stories
Henry IV Part 1
Henry IV Part 2
Henry V
House Made of Dawn
The House of the Seven Gables
Huckleberry Finn
I Know Why the Caged Bird Sings
Ibsen's Plays I
Ibsen's Plays II
The Idiot
Idylls of the King
The Iliad
Incidents in the Life of a Slave Girl
Inherit the Wind
Invisible Man
Ivanhoe
Jane Eyre
Joseph Andrews
The Joy Luck Club
Jude the Obscure

Julius Caesar
The Jungle
Kafka's Short Stories
Keats & Shelley
The Killer Angels
King Lear
The Kitchen God's Wife
The Last of the Mohicans
Le Morte d'Arthur
Leaves of Grass
Les Miserables
A Lesson Before Dying
Light in August
The Light in the Forest
Lord Jim
Lord of the Flies
The Lord of the Rings
Lost Horizon
Lysistrata & Other Comedies
Macbeth
Madame Bovary
Main Street
The Mayor of Casterbridge
Measure for Measure
The Merchant of Venice
Middlemarch
A Midsummer Night's Dream
The Mill on the Floss
Moby-Dick
Moll Flanders
Mrs. Dalloway
Much Ado About Nothing
My Ántonia
Mythology
Narr. …Frederick Douglass
Native Son
New Testament
Night
1984
Notes from the Underground

The Odyssey
Oedipus Trilogy
Of Human Bondage
Of Mice and Men
The Old Man and
the Sea
Old Testament
Oliver Twist
The Once and
Future King
One Day in the Life of
Ivan Denisovich
One Flew Over the
Cuckoo's Nest
100 Years of Solitude
O'Neill's Plays
Othello
Our Town
The Outsiders
The Ox Bow Incident
Paradise Lost
A Passage to India
The Pearl
The Pickwick Papers
The Picture of
Dorian Gray
Pilgrim's Progress
The Plague
Plato's Euthyphro…
Plato's The Republic
Poe's Short Stories
A Portrait of the
Artist…
The Portrait of a Lady
The Power and
the Glory
Pride and Prejudice
The Prince
The Prince and
the Pauper
A Raisin in the Sun
The Red Badge of
Courage
The Red Pony
The Return of the
Native
Richard II
Richard III

The Rise of
Silas Lapham
Robinson Crusoe
Roman Classics
Romeo and Juliet
The Scarlet Letter
A Separate Peace
Shakespeare's
Comedies
Shakespeare's Histories
Shakespeare's
Minor Plays
Shakespeare's Sonnets
Shakespeare's Tragedies
Shaw's Pygmalion &
Arms…
Silas Marner
Sir Gawain…Green
Knight
Sister Carrie
Slaughterhouse-five
Snow Falling on Cedars
Song of Solomon
Sons and Lovers
The Sound and the Fury
Steppenwolf &
Siddhartha
The Stranger
The Sun Also Rises
T.S. Eliot's Poems &
Plays
A Tale of Two Cities
The Taming of the
Shrew
Tartuffe, Misanthrope…
The Tempest
Tender Is the Night
Tess of the D'Urbervilles
Their Eyes Were
Watching God
Things Fall Apart
The Three Musketeers
To Kill a Mockingbird
Tom Jones
Tom Sawyer
Treasure Island &
Kidnapped
The Trial

Tristram Shandy
Troilus and Cressida
Twelfth Night
Ulysses
Uncle Tom's Cabin
The Unvanquished
Utopia
Vanity Fair
Vonnegut's Works
Waiting for Godot
Walden
Walden Two
War and Peace
Who's Afraid of
Virginia…
Winesburg, Ohio
The Winter's Tale
The Woman Warrior
Worldly Philosophers
Wuthering Heights
A Yellow Raft in
Blue Water

Check Out the All-New CliffsNotes Guides

TECHNOLOGY TOPICS
Balancing Your Check-
book with Quicken
Buying and Selling
on eBay
Buying Your First PC
Creating a Winning
PowerPoint 2000
Presentation
Creating Web Pages
with HTML
Creating Your First
Web Page
Exploring the World
with Yahoo!
Getting on the Internet
Going Online with AOL
Making Windows 98
Work for You

Setting Up a
Windows 98
Home Network
Shopping Online Safely
Upgrading and
Repairing Your PC
Using Your First iMac
Using Your First PC
Writing Your First
Computer Program

PERSONAL FINANCE TOPICS
Budgeting & Saving
Your Money
Getting a Loan
Getting Out of Debt
Investing for the
First Time
Investing in
401(k) Plans
Investing in IRAs
Investing in
Mutual Funds
Investing in the
Stock Market
Managing Your Money
Planning Your
Retirement
Understanding
Health Insurance
Understanding
Life Insurance

CAREER TOPICS
Delivering a Winning
Job Interview
Finding a Job
on the Web
Getting a Job
Writing a Great Resume